Archaeology The RaBBis &EarLy Christianity

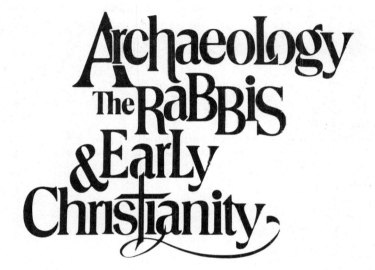

Archaeology The Rabbis & Early Christianity

Eric M. Meyers
& James F. Strange

Abingdon / Nashville

ARCHAEOLOGY, THE RABBIS, AND EARLY CHRISTIANITY:
The Social and Historical Setting of Palestinian
Judaism and Christianity

Copyright © 1981 by Abingdon

Library of Congress Cataloging in Publication Data

MEYERS, ERIC M.
  Archaeology, the rabbis, and early Christianity.
  Bibliography. p.
  Includes index.
  1. Christian antiquities—Palestine. 2. Jews in Palestine—Antiqui-
ties. 3. Palestine—Antiquities. 4. Judaism—History—Greco-Roman
period, 332 B.C.-210 A.D. 5. Christianity—Origin. 6. Bible.
N.T.—Antiquities. I. Strange, James F., joint author. II. Title.
BR133.P3M48   270.1   80-24208

ISBN 0-687-01680-0

MANUFACTURED BY THE PARTHENON PRESS AT
NASHVILLE, TENNESSEE, UNITED STATES OF AMERICA

Contents

CONTENTS

List of Illustrations

Figures

7

Preface

For many years the authors have lamented the absence of a convenient work for both graduate and undergraduate students on the development of early Christianity and Judaism in Palestine as it is informed by the ever-burgeoning discipline of archaeology. There is a gap between literature published for the historical technician (archaeologist) and the historian. Even the new interest in and focus on social history has not led to a resourceful use of nonwritten and nonliterary materials in reconstructing the total matrix of society in this formative era of Western civilization. With this lack in mind, we offer the present study of the Palestinian origins of early Judaism and Christianity.

No attempt is made to be exhaustive or even definitive. Rather, we have striven to suggest the rich, dialogical relation between texts and monuments that exists in Greco-Roman Palestine. What we have to offer here is an introduction to a set of themes that we believe are crucial for a reliable and faithful understanding of the period. The notes are intended as a point of entry for the specialist and the graduate student. In general, however, this work makes available to the student and interested layreader material that is accessible only in Hebrew, Italian, and other foreign languages. In this respect, a good deal of the material presented here should be of use to anyone interested in the fields of early Christianity and the origins of the New Testament, ancient Judaism, and the archaeology of Roman Palestine.

Choosing to be synthetic and selective, the authors have attempted to be both detailed, when circumstances seem to warrant it, and more general, when detail would have obscured the issues. Thus, for example, the languages of Roman Palestine receive far more space than does art. The reader should not infer from this disparity that language is necessarily a better indicator of cultural mood and orientation than are artistic productions. It is of course true, however, that people who study the rabbis and the New Testament are more likely to see the immediate relevance to their disciplines of epigraphic evidence rather than nonepigraphic data such as art. Both in the sections replete with detail and in those that argue more generally, we have not hesitated to state and develop a thesis.

Specifically, this book documents archaeologically and epigraphically the diversity in early Palestinian Judaism that is already well known from ancient literature. Furthermore, we trace the same diversity in early Palestinian Christianity. Heretofore the hypothesis of diversity in pre-Constantinian Christianity was somewhat suspect. This text documents a range of practices and beliefs through archaeology and epigraphy that simply is not clear from ancient literary sources alone.

We also make a case for far more contact between the two communities—Jewish and Christian—than ordinarily has been assumed possible. The authors take the archaeological fact that the holy places of the Jewish and Christian communities operated side by side in Capernaum and Nazareth—two towns associated with the very founding of the ministry of Jesus—as highly suggestive for Jewish-Christian relations. In other words, the reconstruction of Jewish-Christian relations that we gain from archaeological and epigraphic data presents a far more irenic picture than usually has been suspected.

10

Finally, we present a picture of early Jewish and Christian attachment to the land that is diametrically opposed to recent publications on this subject. We insist that there was continuity in local and regional traditions for Christianity as well as for Judaism. That is, even as the Jewish sages focused on the literal as well as spiritual importance of the land of Palestine, so did Christians. We therefore reject the Pella hypothesis, namely, that when Christians fled to Transjordan after the destruction of Jerusalem and the Temple in 70 C.E. they developed a spiritualized concept of the land to replace their former group self-understanding that was tied to Palestine. After all, Christians clearly honored caves and grottoes that they associated with events of holy memory at Nazareth, Capernaum, and Bethany, to name only those sites where we have ample material evidence. The evidence found at these sites indicates a high degree of attachment to the land in Christian circles, an attachment precisely paralleled in Jewish evidences.

That two individuals rather than one have set out to deal with this subject is in itself a statement about the field of Christian origins and the study of early Palestinian Judaism. One has been trained in Hebrew Bible, Jewish history, and archaeology; the other in New Testament, Christian origins, and archaeology. By working together it is hoped that our vision is improved and our individual potential amplified. Ours is a generation without Avi-Yonah and Albright, without Goodenough and Kraeling. These men and many like them have inspired us to go forward with the twofold approach of texts and monuments, books and spades.

The collaboration of the authors in scholarly matters goes back for more than a decade now, and each can say with gratitude and profound indebtedness that the spirit of these exchanges has been exhilarating from the very outset. A challenging and creative collegiality has always marked our relationship. It is no coincidence that our sharing of ideas and mutual nourishment began with the Joint Expedition to Khirbet Shema' and continues with the Meiron Excavation

11

Project, both under the auspices of the American Schools of Oriental Research, which has pioneered all integrative efforts in American biblical circles for nearly a century. We are both deeply grateful to ASOR for providing a common vehicle that has enabled our work in excavation and field survey to go forward these ten years. The inspiration of Ernest Wright, the encouragement of Frank Moore Cross, Jr., and the support of Philip J. King, presidents of ASOR during these years, have been a source of much satisfaction.

But most of all we have profited from the seminars and classes conducted at the Field School on the site of the excavations under the auspices of Duke University Summer School. These experiences brought together faculty and staff from many institutions, along with undergraduates, graduates, and divinity students. The open and frank discussions on all matters relating to the history and archaeology of Palestine in late antiquity have inspired the direction of our thinking and flexibility toward many long-held positions. It was in this context that we listened not only to students but learned to listen to the data itself.

Our colleagues in this learning endeavor who have stimulated our thinking most include A. Thomas Kraabel of the University of Minnesota, Richard Simon Hanson of Luther College, Carol L. Meyers of Duke University, Dennis E. Groh of Garrett-Evangelical Theological Seminary, and Ya' akov Meshorev of the Hebrew University.

The State of Israel, with its lively circle of scholars, teachers, and archaeologists of all nationalities, has proved to be a source of abiding stimulation. It would be difficult to imagine a more supportive atmosphere in which to work.

We hope that the present study contributes in some small measure to the advancement of the integration of history and archaeology in Palestinian studies.

Eric M. Meyers
James F. Strange

CHRONOLOGY

	EGYPT	PALESTINE	SYRIA AND MESOPOTAMIA
525 B.C.E.	Conquest of Persia		Darius I, 522–486
515		Rebuilding of Temple	
		HAGGAI	
		ZECHARIAH	
500		MALACHI c. 500–450	Xerxes I (Ahasuerus), 486
			Artaxerxes I Longimanus, 465
		Ezra, c. 458(?)	Xerxes II, 423
		Nehemiah, 445	Darius II, 423
400		Ezra (again), c. 398(?)	Artaxerxes II Mnemon, 404
			Artaxerxes III, 358
			Arses, 338
		Darius III, 336	

EMPIRE OF ALEXANDER THE GREAT 336–323

	The Ptolemies		*The Kingdom of the Seleucids*
300	Ptolemy I Soter, 323		Seleucus I Nicator, 312
	Ptolemy II Philadelphus, 285		Antiochus I Soter, 280
	Translation of Bible into		Antiochus II Theos, 261
	Greek (LXX) c. 275		Seleucus II Callinicus, 246
			Seleucus III Soter, 226

200

Ptolemies (Egypt)	Jewish History	Seleucids (Syria)
Ptolemy III Euergetes, 246		Antiochus III The Great, 223
Ptolemy IV Philopator, 221		
Ptolemy V Epiphanes, 203	Beginning of the "Pairs" of Teachers, c. 200	Seleucus IV Philopator, 187
	Syrian Conquest 200–198	Antiochus IV Epiphanes, 175
	Qumran, c. 200	
	DANIEL	Antiochus V Eupator, 163
Ptolemy VI Philometer, 181	Maccabean Revolt, 168	Demetrius I Soter, 162
	Judas, 166	Alexander Balas, 150
	Jonathan, 160	
	Simon, 143	Demetrius II Nicator, 145
Ptolemy VII Neos Philopator, 145		Antiochus VI Epiphanes
Ptolemy VIII Euergetes II, 145–116		Dionysius, 145
	John Hyrcanus I, 134	Antiochus VII Sidetes, 139
Ptolemy IX Soter II, 116		Demetrius II Nicator, 129
Ptolemy X Alexander I, 107	Aristobulus I, 104	Cleopatra Thea, 129
	Alexander Jannaeus, 103	Cleopatra Thea and Antiochus VIII Grypus 125–121
Ptolemy XI Alexander II, 80		Seleucus V, 125
Ptolemy XII Neos Dionysos, 80	Salome Alexandra, 76	Roman occupation of Syria, 64–63
	Aristobulus II, 67	
	John Hyrcanus II, 63	

Cleopatra VII Philopator, 51–30
Ptolemy XIII, 51–47
Ptolemy XIV, 47–44

Pompey captures Jerusalem,
Matthias Antigonus, 40–37
Herod the Great, 37–34
Rabbi Hillel and Rabbi
Shammai

	ROMAN EMPEROR	EVENTS IN PALESTINE AND THE EMPIRE
30 B.C.E.	Augustus	Herod begins construction of the Temple
23		Death of Herod the Great, division of his kingdom
4		between Herod Archelaus, Herod Philip, and Herod
		Antipas; birth of Jesus
6 C.E.		Exile of Archelaus and installation of Coponius as first
		Procurator of Judea; the "Census Revolt"
14	Tiberius	Pontius Pilate begins his procuratorship (until 36)
26		Death of Jesus
33		Herod Agrippa I, King of Judea (until 44 C.E.)
37	Gaius Caligula	First Generation of Tannaim
41	Claudius	Beginning of Paul's writing activity
54	Nero	Outbreak of the First Jewish Revolt against Rome
66		Simeon I Patriarch; Second generation of Tannaim
68	Galba	
69	Otho, Vitellius, and Vespasian	

Year	Emperor	Events
70		Destruction of the Temple
73		Fall of Masada (or 74 C.E.)
		MIDDLE ROMAN PERIOD, 73–180 C.E.
		Writing of the canonical gospels
79	Titus	
81	Domitian	
90		Council of Jamnia (Jabneh)
		Second Generation of Tannaim
		Apostolic Fathers
96	Nerva	
98	Trajan	Jewish Unrest under Trajan, 113–117
117	Hadrian	
c. 130		Gamaliel II (in Jabneh; Third Generation of Tannaim)
135		Second Jewish Revolt or the Bar Kokhba Revolt ending in the destruction and refounding of Jerusalem as Aelia Capitolina; Rabbi Akiba active in Palestine
138	Antoninus Pius	
150		Justin Martyr, native of Neapolis in Palestine, debates Trypho in Rome
160		Fourth Generation of Tannaim; Simeon II installed as Patriarch in Galilee
176	Commodus (to 192)	
180		LATE ROMAN PERIOD, 180–324 C.E.
192	Septimus Severus (to 211)	
c. 200	Caracalla (to 217)	
198		Rabbi Judah the Prince, also known as "Rabbi"

209	Origen, the Christian scholar, active in Caesarea
217	Death of Rabbi Judah the Prince, and certification of the Mishnah
218	Elagabalus (to 222)
c. 220	Beginnings of the Amoraim; Gamaliel II is Patriarch
222	Severus Alexander (to 235)
235	Maximinus (to 238)
249	Decius (to 251)
	Foundings of Synagogues in Palestine; Christian persecutions under Decius; beginnings of attestation of Christian caves and grottoes
c. 250	Judah II is Patriarch; Second Generation of Amoraim
253	Valerian (to 260)
270	Gallienus (to 268)
276	Aurelian (to 275)
	Probus (to 282)
c. 280	Gamaliel III Patriarch, Third Generation of Amoraim
284	Diocletian (to 305)
306	Constantine the Great
313	Eusebius becomes Bishop of Caesarea
320	Judah III and Hillel II Patriarchs; Fourth Generation of Amoraim
324	BYZANTINE PERIOD, 324-640 C.E.
	Conversion of Constantine and the "Christianization" of the Empire
325	Council of Nicaea
333	The Bordeaux Pilgrim visits Palestine

Date	Emperor	Event
337	Constans I (to 350)	Death of Constantine; many synagogues rebuilt and renovated in this general period
351		Revolt of the Jews against Gallus Caesar, 351–53
353	Constantius II (to 362)	
c. 360		Gamaliel IV and Judah IV Patriarchs; Fifth Generation of Amoraim
361	Julian (to 363)	Julian's attempt to rebuild the Temple
364	Valens I (to 378)	
379	Valentinian (to 375)	
381	Theodosius (to 383)	Council of Constantinople; Egeria visits Palestine as Pilgrim
383	Arcadius (to 408)	
385		Jerome settles at Bethlehem
393	Honorius (to 423)	
c. 400		Gamaliel VI is Patriarch; close of Amoraic period

1

Introduction:
The Relevance of
Nonliterary Sources

The Scholar of Early
Palestinian Judaism and Nonliterary Sources

Despite the fact that it is nearly a century and a half since Edward Robinson marked the American entrance into Palestinian studies, much that characterized the early years of exploration and publication still remains a fixed part of American scholarship today. That is, a dominant interest in the historical geography and material culture of Eretz Israel has emanated primarily from Old Testament circles. The major twentieth-century figures, Albright, Glueck, and Wright—to mention but a few—while contributing to the overall advancement of Palestinian archaeology, confined their major work to Old Testament biblical sites. In their attempts to define and direct the field of biblical archaeology, however, Albright and Wright particularly broadened their aims by extending the chronological limits of the discipline to include New Testament studies and postbiblical Jewish history.

Still, the primary impetus and sponsorship for fieldwork over the years has derived from divinity schools, which have influenced greatly the direction of an entire discipline. It has been only in the 1970s that the American Schools of Oriental Research (ASOR) has set out systematically to correct this imbalance by helping to sponsor excavations which delve into the areas of Christian origins and early Palestinian Judaism.

The excavation of Khirbet Qumran in the 1950s, together with the subsequent publication of many of its scrolls, has contributed perhaps more than any other single archaeological event to a renewed understanding of the importance of nonliterary remains for the study of the Greco-Roman period in ancient Palestine. Understandably, the scrolls themselves have been the center and focus of scholarly attention, and even those scholars who have accepted their antiquity have often overlooked the fact that it was strictly archaeological data which enabled other historians to verify their age. Careful stratigraphic digging, ceramic and numismatic analysis, and paleographical study, all subdisciplines of the broader archaeological endeavor, combined to constitute a convincing documentation of the early history of the community.

Such a stunning array of new material, ironically, may have created false hopes in the expectation that there will be more of the same. But it should be said quite candidly that such discoveries as the Qumran scrolls are most exceptional, so one cannot simply sit back and wait for new scrolls to be found to clarify historical issues. Most of the new data that have to be taken into account are primarily nonliterary, and only cumulatively will they begin to alter a particular assessment of a given set of problems.

Whatever may be said of the American archaeological bias toward the Old Testament, the time is now ripe for a renewed interest in other periods of the material culture of ancient Palestine. In Israel today local archaeologists and scholars are engaged in fulltime field activities. A very large portion of their results and finds is directly relevant to later periods and will ultimately force a reassessment of older views. It is unfortunate that so much of this activity goes unnoticed and barely filters into discussions about first-century Judaism and Christianity, that is, after the Jewish resistance in the wars against Rome.

Although Israeli scholarship represents a true exception to

the above criticism, it can be said even of segments of that community that nonliterary materials have not significantly influenced certain disciplines there as well, especially rabbinic scholarship. If we turn to the community that produced the edition of the Talmud which has been more or less accepted as normative in the Jewish world of learning, the Babylonian community, we would discover that the finds of Dura-Europos have yet to significantly affect the evaluation of this great Diaspora center of learning. Its magnificent frescoes and unique synagogue belie a cosmopolitan community at the very pulse of Hellenistic civilization of the third century C.E. Moreover, the placement of an apparently well-to-do Jewish community in the center of such a multidimensional society that also included Christians and pagans cannot be accidental.

It was the late E. R. Goodenough who effectively brought home the importance of Dura to Jewish studies and students of the early church as well as the more general artifactual repertoire of materials from the Greco-Roman period. Goodenough did not have the impact he had hoped for because of his rather inflexible integrating hypothesis that such materials were the key to understanding a mystical type of Judaism which Philo of Alexandria had presaged. He believed that most of the writing of Babylonian Jews had been edited out of the tradition and that only the artifacts left behind could help us better understand the corresponding cultural developments. Such a dichotomous view of the world of the sages has been effectively challenged in many quarters today and has forced upon students of the rabbinic field the continuing and difficult question of what the true import of such things as zodiacs and griffins, conchs and winged victories, and Medusas and scenes from pagan mythology really was when found in the tombs and synagogues of Palestinian and Diaspora Jews. Even though no real consensus has emerged, all who work with such data are forever indebted to Goodenough for at least opening up the broader methodological question of how to include artifactual

21

data in evaluating the developments within early Judaism and the church.

One of the great difficulties to have resulted from Goodenough's massive thirteen-volume work, however, has been the dependency of English readers upon it. We have mentioned the organizing hypothesis around which he builds a case for a Hellenized, Philonic Judaism paving the way for the rapid spread and early Hellenization of Christianity. It should be emphasized, moreover, that Goodenough was not an archaeologist and so did not critically assay the evidence he used with any chronological precision. For example, many of the artifacts he discusses fit more properly into the Byzantine period than into the Roman period. The fact that many libraries shelve his magnum opus in the reference section has contributed to the misleading impression that his work is authoritative and reliable in this regard.

A major consideration in the preparation of this text has been the fact that there does not exist a handy and reliable survey for students of the Greco-Roman period which takes into account the extraordinary strides made in the archaeological world since Goodenough commenced and concluded his monumental study. The purpose, therefore, of this book is primarily to alert the serious reader to the fact that the problems confronting the historian of Judaism or Christianity are considerably more complex today because of the existence of new data that simply must be evaluated and studied on a serious level.

The Scholar of the
New Testament and Nonliterary Sources

In the last decade, it has largely been theological concerns that have characterized New Testament research. Although investigation of historical matters has not disappeared, such inquiry has often remained the domain of the popularizer rather than of the original scholar. In certain quarters there has even been a tendency to relegate the New Testament documents to the domain of theology to the exclusion of history or geography. This extreme position is most commonly, though not entirely fairly, associated with the writings of Rudolf Bultmann. Yet it is still commonplace in New Testament study to understand the purpose of the New Testament writers as theological rather than historical.

Although a theological intent by the various authors of New Testament literature cannot be denied, it is also true that the New Testament exhibits a historical context or contexts. That is, this collection of writings has a history of its own. It presupposes a historical situation, not a historical vacuum. Recognition of this historical setting comes to expression in modern scholarship as "the science of New Testament introduction" or perhaps "New Testament background." Scholars may even specialize in this subdiscipline. Alternative avenues of scholarship may also include "the history of New Testament times" and the various social histories (e.g., social history of early Christianity, social history of Gentile Christianity). Nevertheless, the rubric "archaeology of the New Testament" or even "New Testament archaeology" is not normally recognized as a specialization within the wider discipline of New Testament scholarship, even though the parallel phenomenon in Old Testament studies has a long and honorable history.

"But what can we learn about New Testament backgrounds from archaeology that we cannot learn from ancient literature?" asks the New Testament scholar. "After all, we have Josephus and a multitude of ancient authors to draw from in reconstructing the history of the period." First and perhaps most important, one needs to be aware at the outset that the aims of archaeology today include as complete a reconstruction of the total culture and history of a people as possible. Years ago the aims of archaeology were much more modest and manageable. In those days one merely described and presented the finds from a given site. Thus R. A. S.

23

Macalister, who dug for years at Gezer, and also at Jerusalem, published three large volumes describing and presenting his findings, but made no overall interpretation in the modern sense. Because of this the Old Testament scholar has been hard put to use the finds from Gezer for illumination of biblical history since a total cultural and historical understanding of this important biblical city was not available. The extensive work at Gezer in the 1960s and 1970s conducted under the auspices of Hebrew Union College has enabled modern scholarship to go forward with that task now. Indeed, the Gezer excavations have proven to be a common training ground for many of America's leading field archaeologists.

Today archaeologists are filling in details of commerce, daily life, religion, and political affairs in our total historical understanding that may have surprisingly important implications for understanding the immediate world of the New Testament. This in turn cannot but have far-reaching implications for understanding the social history of early Palestinian Judaism. Furthermore, a grasp of the world and audience of the early Christian movement will surely eventuate in new exegetical understandings of the text of the New Testament itself.

Perhaps a brief survey of some of the newer historical and cultural understandings of the text of the New Testament world would be useful here. For example, one might point to the reign of Herod the Great as a period whose history is greatly enlarged in important ways by the findings of archaeology. Josephus does not appear to depict Herod in a positive light as a Jew, particularly since Herod built pagan temples dedicated to Augustus at Caesarea and Sebaste as well as many other temples elsewhere. Yet his own fortresses of Herodium (near Bethlehem) and Masada (on the south and west shores of the Dead Sea) are devoid of iconography. In other words, though one might believe from reading Josephus that Herod was simply an opportunist in religion, the remains of his isolated fortresses might support the view that he was an observing Jew in private, at least in terms of the second commandment. It is even possible to argue that he supported synagogue Judaism privately because a synagogue has been found built into the casemate wall of Masada. Not all archaeologists and historians would agree to this reading of archaeological evidence. Nevertheless, these data cannot be ignored in any attempt to assess Herod and his reign.

While we are speaking of Herod, it is important to mention evidence from the Second Temple, built by Herod and uncovered by Israeli archaeologists beginning in 1967. Although only the huge precinct surrounding this temple can now be excavated, it is safe to say from these excavations alone that the sentence in the Gospel of Luke that the temple was adorned with beautiful stones and votive offerings (21:5) is an understatement. As reconstructed by the expedition architects, the Royal Portico above the south wall of the precinct was overwhelming indeed, both in terms of size and beauty. This massive wall was decorated, according to the archaeological evidence, with panels, friezes, and other stone elements carved in elaborate geometrical and floral patterns. Furthermore, excavations south of the enormous precinct wall revealed a monumental stairway about sixty-four meters wide that led to the Huldah Gates and thence under the Royal Portico to the inner court of the temple. This is possibly the entrance used by Peter and John in Acts 3 to the gate "called Beautiful." The Double Gate in the south wall answers this description, being decorated with columns and domes and plasterwork in Eastern Hellenistic style. The Royal Portico, incidentally, is a good candidate for the site of "the cleansing of the temple" recorded in all four Gospels. It is also a strong possibility for the site where Jesus stood teaching "in the temple."

Traces of a gate at the southwest corner of the Herodian city wall, together with remains of possibly first-century ritual baths in the vicinity, have invited a controversial reconstruction of an "Essene Quarter" in Jerusalem on what is now

Mount Zion.[1] If this reconstruction is correct, it may help explain the events of Acts 2.

At Capernaum we can find archaeological data relevant to the early ministry of Jesus. Excavations there have unearthed what fourth-century Christians surely thought of as Peter's house, judging from their graffiti scratched in the plaster of the house after it was rebuilt as a church. Since the house was founded in the first century C.E., it is possible that the Gospels' mention of Jesus living at the house of Simon Peter (or Peter and Andrew) finds realization here. Even if the convictions of fourth-century Christians are fantasies, it is possible to show archaeologically that Capernaum was a large village at least partially supported by fishing. Its inhabitants built mainly single-story courtyard houses of local black basalt. They were not rich, but neither were they poor. That is to say, the archaeological remains of the site suggest that the community lived comfortably, enjoying a plenteous food supply and the benefits of a community whose reputation as a pilgrim center was just beginning to have its full effect on village life. In fact, from the finds it is possible to suggest that Capernaum was a teeming Jewish commercial and agricultural center. Perhaps it was a natural selection for Jesus' headquarters.

On the other hand, Magdala and Tiberias to the west and south seem to have been more Romanized (and perhaps paganized?) than Capernaum or Chorazin, judging from the architectural remains. This is not without implications in terms of understanding the nature of Jesus' ministry, namely, that he came to the "lost sheep of the house of Israel" (Matt. 10:6 and elsewhere), which perhaps accounts for the lack of a mention of any visit by Jesus to either locality.

It has been suggested in the past that Jesus came from a Hellenized area and from a crossroads town. This hypothesis purports to explain the universalism of his message. There is a narrow sense in which archaeology supports this old contention in that there is evidence now that the Judaism of Lower Galilee was far more open to the Hellenizing influences

26

of the coastal cities than Upper Galilee. On the other hand, Jesus' insistence that his mission was to Israel alone implies that his is a more conservative stance. Excavations at Nazareth tend to support the view that this was not an open city but a tiny agricultural village not far off the beaten path and, indeed, close to the major trade routes. There is no iconography or pagan symbolism to support a syncretistic hypothesis. In fact, if anything, the archaeology tends to support Nathanael's negative attitude toward Nazareth recorded in the Gospel of John (1:46), since it appears to have been such an unpretentious place. On the other hand, we have literary evidence that one of the twenty-four priestly courses settled here after 70 C.E., which implies that the remnants of temple Judaism found Nazareth "clean" and unsullied by paganism.

There is much more that could be said by way of introduction to the problem of New Testament studies and archaeology. We will only mention here certain questions that have implications for the former and for which important nonliterary evidence is in hand. These problems include the dominant language of Judaism, the attitude toward iconography on the part of the Jews, the extent of Hellenization of Palestine, the religiosity of the people (as opposed to "official" synagogue or temple religion), the extent of literacy in first-century Judaism, the social milieu of Jerusalem and other cities in the first century, and the pattern of Jewish life in the Diaspora visited by Paul.

Much of this boils down to an identification of the type of Judaism represented by Jesus, the apostles, and the New Testament writers who are Jewish. Some would rephrase this to the question of the religiosity of these men, but the analysis remains the same. Since we have no direct archaeological evidence relating to these figures (outside of the House of Saint Peter in Capernaum, which is still debated), we are bound to use indirect evidence. This evidence is both literary and nonliterary. In a sense, the archaeological evidence is the most honest of all, for the paraphernalia of everyday life is manufactured for one's personal needs, not for one's audience. Therefore it would be a serious error to exclude archaeological and other nonliterary evidence in reconstructing the history and culture of the period. Each type of data serves as a useful corrective for the other.

The Limits of Archaeology

Archaeology alone can be very helpful in the interpretation of ancient texts. First, it can supplement the ancient record, that is, it can provide information not contained within texts. Indeed, when it comes to the synagogues of ancient Palestine, much of the data comes from famous sites, such as Baram, which are not even remembered in the literary record. Along these lines, most of the artifactual data of synagogues dates from the end of the amoraic period, in short, later than the major literary sources which deal with their functioning. It would seem foolhardy, therefore, for a serious scholar to ignore material evidence in any consideration of early Palestinian Judaism. The same holds true for many of the early churches of Palestine: many simply lack any literary pedigree whatsoever.

Second, archaeological data can greatly facilitate the exegetical task that seeks to bring greater clarity to obscure texts or to increase one's understanding of a difficult passage. A careful study of Jewish burial customs and the vocabulary associated with them may illuminate both difficult talmudic and New Testament passages. A study of secondary loculus burials, for example, helps us to understand the seemingly anomalous practice of Jewish reburial into bone boxes, or ossuaries, and hence enables us to understand more fully the Mishnaic passage having to do with the wasting away of the flesh and the joy of reburial *(Moed Qatan* 1.5). Similarly, the examination of Jesus' tomb several days after the crucifixion is given a new and more realistic reading when accompanied by a detailed study of Jewish tombs. Finally, archaeological reconstruction of ancient roofing methods helps us understand how the men carrying the paralytic could lower him through the roof to Jesus (Mark 2:4).

Third, archaeology can and does often contradict the written text, or appears to be in conflict with it. An openness to the evidence of archaeology enables one therefore at least to recognize the limitations of the written record in some regards. It now may be documented that all synagogues are not built on the highest spot (e.g., Khirbet Shema', Gush Halav, lower synagogue), as is the indicated practice in the Tosepta (*Megilla* 4.23). Likewise, there are no archaeological remains about sixty stadia from Jerusalem as a candidate for ancient Emmaus (Luke 24:13).

Fourth, it is also true that archaeology can do more than assist in understanding rabbinic or New Testament texts: it can confirm their reliability as well and establish the veracity of historical information preserved within them. Excavations at Nazareth tend to legitimate the apparently ironic comment of Nathanael, who was from Cana near Nazareth (John 1:46). The excavations of Jerusalem provide us with a detailed sense of the urban grandeur of the Holy City. Synagogue excavations provide us with vivid documentation of the major factor influencing their architectural design, namely, the principle of sacred orientation toward Jerusalem (Dan. 6:10; Tos. *Megilla* 4.22; *b. Berakot* 30a and Josephus *Against Apion* 2.10).

The present work is an attempt to sensitize students of early Palestinian Judaism and Christianity to the importance of using archaeology as well as ancient texts in their basic approach to these important historical periods. Texts alone cannot help us resolve the many issues that still confront entire fields of research. While it would be brash to think that archaeology alone can help remedy such a situation, it is not overly optimistic to think that a multidimensional approach which utilizes texts and monuments together will go a long way toward making new inroads into old material.

29

It is important, however, to underscore again the limits of archaeology, for the archaeologist is really first and foremost a supplier of raw material for historical research. Some of these raw materials will be written, epigraphic remains, but more often than not, the data the researcher will have to interpret will be nothing more than walls and other parts of a structure whose dating will be in dispute, or possibly some graffiti on a piece of plaster from a tomb whose ownership is in doubt. But this is the kind of data that ultimately sets the lives and teachings of human beings in their true contexts. Such data may also tell us a good deal about the impact of humans on their fellow beings or of their impact on the environment. No serious history student or scholar today would dare set out to study the medieval period without at least knowing in a rudimentary way the barest essentials of Gothic architecture and medieval art. So it is for the ancient period as well, for it is only when we pit real people up against their real historical situations that we can ever hope to recover their true social, economic, and religious settings. Texts and monuments are but two routes to the recovery of historical actuality. Sooner or later these routes must intersect, and only then will we be closer to the world we endeavor so hard to recreate.

2

The Cultural Setting of Galilee:
The Case of Regionalism and Early
Palestinian Judaism

Methodological Considerations

Assuming the twofold methodological approach outlined in
the previous chapter, it is now apparent that scholars today
are in the enviable position of being able to evaluate the data
of entire regions and areas within ancient Palestine. Such a
regional approach to archaeology has been used most
effectively in Israel by the late Yochanan Aharoni and his staff
in the pioneering researches of the Beersheba region of the
Negev. Attempting to understand better the transition from
the Bronze Age to the Iron Age and the patriarchal period,
systematic excavation of a string of sites was begun in regular
alternation with field survey. Aharoni conceived of this tactic
as a student while preparing for his doctorate when he
systematically surveyed large areas of the *galil* hoping to learn
more about the early Israelite settlement there.[1] His
comprehensive regional approach to historical and archaeological research has been embraced and carried on by his
followers at Tel Aviv University.

While such an approach has been more or less common in
New World archaeological/anthropological circles for some
time, it has not yet sufficiently influenced the field of
Syro-Palestinian studies to have produced striking new
results. What we shall attempt to do here, therefore, must be

31

regarded as a somewhat provisional sort of synthesis of our recent work in northern Galilee.[2] Despite such a demurrer, we believe that even now it is possible to bring an entirely new perspective on Galilean studies in general as a result of nearly a decade of work. Our major focus is "early Palestinian Judaism" rather than "primitive," or "nascent Christianity," because our methodologies have thus far inhibited us from positively identifying more than a few early Christian sites prior to Constantine the Great. While several scholars have argued convincingly for the presence of an indigenous Palestinian Jewish-Christianity in the Early Roman period (50 c.e.–70 c.e.), especially the Italian Franciscans,[3] the present authors are unable to accept their identification of the so-called Jewish-Christian repertoire of symbols in this formative period.

Surely there is important work to be done on the subject of early Jewish-Christianity, or Palestinian Christianity, in Galilee. But until such time as we are able to identify and relate sites and artifacts to a specific religious community, we shall not succeed in discussing pre-Constantinian Christianity from the archaeological-literary perspective we have argued for—save for the kind of material discussed in the next chapter. At the very least, the paucity of pre-Constantinian Christian remains forces us to be aware of a potentially more complex set of data than we presently are willing to admit. Could all the early Christians have fled to Pella in Transjordan during or after the first Jewish war against Rome between 66–73 c.e.? Surely such could not have been the case.[3a] Rather it is reasonable to expect that many simply fled northward with their fellow Jews to sink new roots in the historical locus of a major part of Jesus' ministry. Indeed, the existence of a Jewish-Christian presence in Palestine is presupposed by the rabbinic writings which identify the *minim* of the Talmud as Jewish Christians.[3b]

So it is with this kind of historical openness that we commence our consideration of the nature of the Galilean community as we may reconstruct it from both archaeology and literature. While recent years have given birth to several new long-term publication projects which, in many respects, begin to fill a large vacuum in the scholarly literature,[4] both American and continental European scholars have avoided the archaeology of the later periods in their prolific writings on New Testament, rabbinica, and church history. It can be said quite unhesitatingly that today, and for some time in the future, Israeli scholars will continue to dominate the field, and they will no doubt continue to publish primarily in Hebrew and largely in the form of preliminary reports that are not widely disseminated.[5] There is, in short, a crying need for scholars to see and study recent archaeological findings which include osteological, zoological, faunal, and botanical remains as well as *objets d'art,* inscriptions, ceramics, and architectural materials, because all are important cultural indicators. A bias in favor of literary sources still predominates in the study of late antiquity in Palestine. It is certainly not true that all that is needed to rectify this situation is new excavations, though there is no doubt they will help. What seems to be indicated, rather, is a reorientation of existing disciplines to the study of material culture. The methods used can take many forms.

Surface survey and exploration is one possibility, and the present study is in part an outgrowth of one such modest venture. The project began in 1973 as part of a seminar on Christian origins sponsored by Hebrew Union College, the Union of American Hebrew Congregations, and Duke University. It was called "The Origins of Christianity: Archaeological and Literary Sources," and surface survey was made an integral part of careful stratigraphic excavation. The survey aspect of this work helped orient the authors and the excavation team itself toward larger regional concerns. Especially helpful was the ceramic material that was collected for comparative analysis.[6] The major difficulty with surface material, however, is that it is unstratified and hence can only be tied into a ceramic typology that has already been established. Another problem is that materials found on the surface usually derive from the latest periods of occupation, namely the Byzantine, Arabic, and even Crusader periods. Hence at most ruins Hellenistic or Early Roman material is scarce on the surface but quite regularly found in excavation.

While one of the predominating concerns of the authors has been the recovery of data that would help reconstruct Galilee of the first century C.E., it has become abundantly clear that a large body of material from this period may never become available. One reason for this is that the resettlement of Jews, and possibly of Christians, from the south in the first and second centuries C.E. caused destruction (archaeologically speaking) of many of the earlier remains. The overwhelming bulk of all materials, both architectural and other, coming out of Galilee thus dates from the Middle-Late Roman period and later, that is the second to fourth centuries C.E. There is no doubt about the importance of such data per se, but it does confront us with the all-important methodological problem of deriving cultural or historical inferences from later materials and relating them to an earlier setting. In the meantime, however, even the limited amount of early data can permit us to make some limited observations. The issue will be answered conclusively only when, after considerable excavation, a large enough corpus of early material is finally available for evaluation. While such an undertaking is truly formidable, the publication of several important new excavations can change the current state of affairs in a very short time.

Such data is provided by the recent work in Judaea and Samaria, and especially in Jerusalem, which has indicated a standard of living for the first century hitherto known mainly from literary sources. Even though much of the evidence clearly reinforces the picture of Jerusalem that we have from literature, some of the material raises substantive issues in specific areas such as population estimates, degree of accommodation to Hellenism, topography, burial customs, the manner of crucifixion, and the extent and nature of buildings in Jerusalem of the Second Temple period.[7] The possibility of further excavation in the *galil*, though we cannot expect such spectacular results, will go a long way toward resolving some of the many issues in Galilean studies which one day must be faced. The recent excavation of Magdala (Tarichaeae) by the Italians and our own work at en-Nabratein have greatly raised our expectations for Galilee.

Historical Issues in Galilean Studies

One purpose of the present study is to indicate how a broadened archaeological approach to the history of Galilee will enable us to understand better many of the unresolved historical problems that have lingered in the literature. For example, the persistence of certain views which might best be described as deriving from a sort of geographical determinism, such as the view that Galilee had special theological significance in the messianic scheme of things, requires an evaluation in light of topograhical and archaeolcgical study.[8] Thus far such views are usually challenged on literary grounds exclusively. If the Galilee of Jesus was *sui generis,* as the distinguished contemporary scholar Geza Vermes has claimed in his *Jesus the Jew,*[9] then it follows that one must strive to understand not only the literary sources which may describe such a state but also the material culture in which such a point of view might have flourished. If we are ever truly to understand the force of the expression "Jesus of Nazareth" then we must adopt an approach which takes into account the cultural factors operative in the Galilee of that period or just after. The term "Jesus the Galilean" appears to be the creation of modern scholarship which has frequently sought to understand Jesus in his special Galilean context.

However, searching the Gospels for clear geographical clues is in the main a very frustrating task, since they are, on the one hand, presented by a community removed nearly two generations from the main events they describe and, on the other hand, preserved by early Christians whose relations with the Jewish community were very strained.[10] W. D. Davies has argued recently that by 70–90 C.E. Christianity had so spiritualized the territorial doctrine of the land that precise details about topographic or geographic elements are lacking in the New Testament.[11] Similarly, the reliance by many Jewish scholars on late sources about Galilee, not to mention their frequent reliance on very limited sources to argue that only a shallow kind of religious life flourished there, is of questionable methodological value.[12] What is intended here is not a refutation of previously held views on the nature of Galilean Judaism at the turn of the era and in the first centuries but rather a presentation of a new and broader approach, which takes into account several lines of inquiry into these large and familiar blocks of material, and a suggestion of a collateral way to address this issue.

A significant new study by Aharon Oppenheimer on the *'am ha-aretz*[13] argues convincingly that the diversity which characterized Judaea in Second-Temple times is paralleled in Galilee and continues well on into tannaitic (or early rabbinic) times in Galilee as well. His particular point of departure is the "people of the land," the *'am ha-aretz,* who have been identified as Christians or Samaritans by some or simply as those ignorant Jews cut off from the mainstream by others. In any case, many scholars have sought to identify them as Galilean Jews of the simplest kind, from whose ranks Jesus emerged with great support. Oppenheimer shows quite clearly that while such issues as ritual purity and tithes clearly separated the *'ammei ha-aretz* from their fellow Jews in some ways, these issues did not in the least inhibit their social interaction with many other kinds of Jews, and that the *'ammei ha-aretz* were as common to Judaea as to Galilee. In fact, he says there is a good deal of continuity between north and south if we accept the fact of great diversity being common to both areas.[14]

A broadened approach to the study of Galilee must therefore take into account this diversity which is reflected in both archaeological and literary sources. Ultimately, both the rabbinic specialist and the New Testament scholar will have to investigate their literary traditions in the context of the specific geographic areas for which they emerge.[15] It stands to reason that the Palestinian Talmud is a more reliable guide to Palestinian everyday life and to the rulings of that community than the Babylonian Talmud. Similarly, New Testament documents of Palestinian provenance should reflect more accurately the setting from which they derive.

The challenge E. R. Goodenough laid before us thus still goes unanswered. Students of Greco-Roman Palestine continue to go about their studies the same way they did generations ago. Even if Goodenough is far off the mark in understanding the colorful synagogue mosaics of the Rift Valley—with their human and animal representations—as presupposing a sort of Hellenistic mysticism set apart from and opposite the rabbis, he has left us with the task of relating all the material culture to a variegated and richly diverse rabbinic Judaism.

Assuming for the moment, therefore, that there was social stratification and diversity within early Palestinian Judaism and that it extended into Galilee, we must express some hesitance in accepting the popularly held view that Galilee was characterized most by ignorance of the law and by a spontaneous sort of religious life which yearned and sought after miracles and the holy men who wrought them. In that view Yochanan ben Zakkai's dictum "Galilee, Galilee, thou hatest the Torah" becomes the catchphrase for understanding Jewish religious phenomena there, and the 'am ha-aretz becomes the paradigmatic figure in explaining the dynamics of the emergence of early Christianity. Were such a division of religious groupings into distinct regions a reality in the first century, we would have expected Flavius Josephus, one not at all hesitant to level criticism or describe sectarians, to provide some support for that view. Josephus, however, pictures Galilee as consisting mainly of Torah-true Jews and does not hint at all that Galilee spawned its own sort of assimilated Judaism.[16] The silence of Josephus on this matter, therefore, seems to be one of the most compelling reasons for rejecting an exclusively Galilean locus for the *'am ha-aretz*.

The very fact that after the First Revolt (66–73 C.E.) Jews from the south so easily integrated into and so readily became acclimatized to northern Palestine suggests a far greater continuity between the religious communities of these areas. Nonetheless, our research has provided us with much new material to evaluate "all the land of Galilee," which perhaps can help us to view better this vital transition in Jewish history. One of the most important ways we may improve our perspective on the religious and cultural factors operating in Galilee is by studying the historical geography of the area. By doing this, it will soon become clear that to view Galilee as one region with one culture is simply no longer possible.

Topography as a Factor in Understanding Galilee

Our point of departure in this section is the reintroduction of Josephus's twofold division of Galilee into Upper Galilee[17] and Lower Galilee.[18] The Mishnah adds to this Tiberias.[19] Together, these sources provide us with sufficient data to argue that it is very difficult to speak of Galilee as a single entity,[20] a fact clearly verified as one comes to grips with the physical realities of the land itself. Once we are able to observe the division of the north into distinct regions, then we are in a far better position (a) to evaluate the evidence found within each of these areas, (b) to reexamine the literary corpus for traces of special meaning alluded to here and there, and (c) to compare and relate the data from one area to that of the next. It also stands to reason that such territorial divisions are bound to have had profound influences on the material culture of the north in general, if not upon the entire socioeconomic and social-religious picture. In addition, the Mishnah describes Galilee as follows:

> Three countries are to be distinguished in what concerns the law of Removal: Judaea, beyond Jordan and Galilee; and each of them is divided into three lands. [Galilee is divided into] upper Galilee, lower Galilee, and the valley: from Kefar Hanania upwards, wheresoever sycamores do not grow, is upper Galilee; from Kefar Hanania downwards, wheresoever sycamores grow, is lower Galilee; the region of Tiberias is the valley.[21]

Consequently, in our discussions we shall refer to *Lower* Galilee as that territory whose western boundary is defined by the slopes of Mount Carmel and whose eastern boundary is mainly marked by the Sea of Galilee. On the south the line follows the Nazareth fault to Mount Tabor, where it turns north to the southern tip of the Sea of Galilee. The northern boundary is marked by the southern slopes of Mount Meiron at the sites of Kefar Hananiah (Kefar Inan) and Beersheba North (Bersabe) in the Beth ha-Kerem Valley.[22] The hills of Lower Galilee, though they inhibited north-south communication to some extent, did not inhibit a lively trade with the Mediterranean and Sea of Galilee. Not only were major trans-Galilee routes established around the lateral valleys of Lower Galilee, but branches as well.[23]

On the other hand, *Upper* Galilee, referred to as "Tetracomia" (Four Villages) by Josephus, is a self-enclosed area defined by the awesome slopes of the Meiron massif.[24] The territory extends northward into the foothills of the Lebanon range, reaching westward to Peqi'in, or the boundary with Akko-Ptolemais.[25] Its eastern extremity extends to the Jordan Valley. This region is approximately 180 miles square, over against Lower Galilee, which is roughly 470 miles square. Adjacent to Upper Galilee are situated the Golan Heights, or ancient Gaulanitis, defined in its northern extremity by the border with the city territory of Caesarea Philippi (Banias) and in the south by that of Hippos-Susitha.[26]

By virtue of sheer topography, Gaulanitis is strongly tied to northern and northeastern Galilee.

The geographic situation as just described is heavily dependent on the reconstruction of Avi-Yonah and does not follow Josephus uncritically. Especially lacking in detail in Josephus is the Upper Galilee–Tyre frontier,[27] which does not play a significant role in his writing and may suggest that the northeast limits of Galilee reach as far as Tyre itself. The only place that occupies his attention is Gischala (Gush Halav), which is the base of his zealot rival, John son of Levi.[28] Due mainly to the fact that Josephus had to concentrate his forces in Lower Galilee on the campaigns against Vespasian and Titus, he managed to fortify only four villages in Upper Galilee, namely, Acchabaron, Seph, Jamnith, and Mero (Meiron).[29]

If we look at the so-called zealot hypothesis[30] from the point of view of Galilean geography, we will notice that many of the important zealot areas cluster in Upper Galilee, especially in the territory adjacent to Tyre. Josephus refers to this smaller region as "Chabulon."[31] We have already rejected any notion of geographic determinism, but if we look at Upper Galilee as an excellent area of refuge set apart by reasons of topography, notably the Meiron massif, then we can better understand why certain events took place there and not elsewhere. For example, it was in these rocky hills that Jesus the brigand chief was hired to wrest the Galilean command from Josephus;[32] that John of Gischala plundered much of Galilee;[33] that Varus sent troops from Ptolemais to subdue rebellious groups;[34] and that Cestius, governor of Syria, marched into the area of Chabulon.[35]

It would be misleading, however, to push the zealot hypothesis is too far, in view of the fact that nearly the entire Jewish population in the decades before the First War joined hands in opposing Rome. Some villages joined the war effort in order to defend themselves against the attacks of Roman and Greek residents of Palestine (*War* 2.457-86; *Life* 27). The populace also rallied to reconquer cities that had fallen out of Jewish control (*War* 3.9). In the words of David Rhoads:

> There was a readiness in Galilee, except at Sepphoris and Tiberias, to fortify for the return of the Romans (*War* 3.40-41). And although many fled the rural areas in the face of the Roman legions, the Galilean troops took their stand in the cities which had been fortified in the brief time they had to prepare for Vespasian's appearance. There was representative resistance in each territory of the nation, as exemplified by the readiness of the popular militia from Idumaea to oppose any attempt of the national leaders to surrender.[36]

Nonetheless, supportive of the idea that Upper Galilee functioned as sort of a refuge area from the earliest time of its settlement are the clusters of villages very close to one another. In the Meiron area, for example, the following Jewish villages are known either through surveys or published data: Khirbet Shema' (Teqo 'a), Gush Halav, Sasa, Ein es-Sumei, Farod, Kefar Hananiah, Bersabe (Beersheba North), Qadesh, Nabratein, Dalton, Alma, and Qatsyon. Of the villages mentioned in the list of the twenty-four priestly courses, Tsefat and Yamnit (possibly to be identified with either Khirbet Yamma or Khirbet Ein Honi) appear to be located in the general area. There is a similar clustering of localities along the Rift Valley and the Sea of Galilee: in the north Chorazin, Capernaum, Magdala (Tarichaeae), Wadi Hamam (Arbel, two sites); Tiberias (Hammath and others), Beth Shean, Rehov, Kochav ha-Yarden, to the south. This clustering of Jewish towns continues on the eastern side of the Sea of Galilee to an approximate inland distance of ten kilometers. Mentioning only a few of the better-known settlements, we might list Hammath Gader, Fik Dabbura, Qaysrein (Caesarea?), Ein Nashut, Husfiyeh, Umm el-Qannatir, Kanaf, Yahudiyeh, and many others. Since published reports from Gaulanitis are so limited, we await further publication to bring the list of Jewish sites to more than thirty. The layout of all these areas is similar; they lie within a band approximately ten kilometers west and east of the Sea of Galilee. In both Galilee and Golan, beyond this invisible line pagan and Christian sites are in evidence, and all seem to share in a common culture.[37]

While it is true that the lag in publication inhibits our detailed understanding of these areas, it is not too soon to offer a new hypothesis for interpreting in a preliminary way much of this important data. Both Avi-Yonah[38] and Baly[39] have argued that only Lower Galilee of all the northern territories remained under the effective control of Rome during the Roman period. Upper Galilee on the other hand—and we would add to this western Golan—remained less affected by Roman foreign policy and, in particular, urbanization. Avi-Yonah goes even further when he suggests that particularly Upper Galilee was less affected by the ever-growing Greco-Roman culture.[40] The question then arises whether the transfer of Jewish settlements to Upper Galilee after the Roman wars was motivated by a desire to escape close contact with Roman and pagan culture or whether it was the result of geography. Moreover, if we can document that Jewish material culture in this mountainous refuge area is different from that of Lower Galilee and finds its closest parallel in the Golan, what historical implications or inferences might be drawn from such data? Josephus himself speaks of Sepphoris (and Arav-Qadarah?), Tiberias, and Tarichaeae as the major cities of Lower Galilee as opposed to the villages of Upper Galilee (Tetracomia). When he says "cities" he probably means toparchies, but the very fact that there are none in Upper Galilee indicates a different, less rigid administrative arrangement.[41]

In trying to assess the importance of this information for a better understanding of the social and religious atmosphere of the Early Roman period, we must always keep in mind these topographic realities. The cities, or toparchies, of Lower Galilee are all tied into the important trade routes that connect the Sea of Galilee with the coastal plain: Tiberias is best reached by the Wadi Tir' an, which leads to Sepphoris; Tarichaeae connects with the Wadi Arbel, which in turn links with the Wadi Beth Natuf leading south of Haifa; and the sites of Chorazin and Capernaum ultimately are connected with Akko-Ptolemais via Wadi Beth ha-Kerem. All these Lower Galilean sites are thus urbane centers linked to the more pagan and hence Greek-speaking West, with its cosmopolitan atmosphere and multilingual population. Topography also enables us to locate the bulk of Jesus' career in Lower Galilee (Nazareth, Nain, and Cana) and in the Rift Valley region, with headquarters in Capernaum.[42] The isolation often associated with the Galilean personality is therefore quite inappropriate when we speak of Jesus of Nazareth, who grew up along one of the branches of one of the busiest trade routes of ancient Palestine, the Way of the Sea (Via Maris). This minor branch became prominent as the significance of nearby Sepphoris grew when in Roman times it became one of the most important administrative centers of the Roman provincial government. Furthermore, Nazareth occupied a commanding position overlooking the route of the Via Maris itself through the Jezreel Valley. Similarly, Yochanan ben Zakkai, reputed to have spent eighteen formative years at Arav near Sepphoris in Lower Galilee,[43] could hardly have been isolated from the major currents of either the Jewish intellectual world or the non-Jewish world, as some rabbinic sources seem to suggest.

The real question is whether anyone in Lower Galilee who lived in so busy an area could have escaped the dominant cultural tendencies of that region. While many small towns here and there in both Galilees—possibly Arav—surely flourished, could they have escaped the kind of broader cultural influences at work? Indeed, could the sages themselves ignore an area of such vital importance? A case of topographic isolation, and hence cultural isolation, therefore cannot easily be made for Lower Galilee. On the contrary, only the geographic realities of Upper Galilee permit such a theory of isolation, and as we note below, even this notion must be revised as a result of recent numismatic finds in that area. The negative reflections of many of the later sages on Galilee[44] may be due to the isolation of the extreme north or even perhaps to the degree to which Hellenistic culture was encroaching upon the south of Galilee. The latter state is amply attested to in the data from the necropolis at Beth She' arim, where pagan artistic motifs and Greek language play a dominant role.[45] It thus seems that at the very least we must take more seriously the twofold division of Galilee attested to in literary sources. As we come in subsequent chapters to sketch the apparent diversity of influences operative in material culture, we should keep open also the possibility of similar phenomena occurring in the literary traditions.

Avi-Yonah has explained that the cities of Palestine took a pacifying role during the First Roman War and so the administrative reorganization afterward was merely an attempt "to extend the municipal system over as wide an area as possible."[46] Both Upper Galilee and the Golan remained outside the municipal system after the war, and the smaller villages located in these regions were

grouped into adminstrative districts ruled by representatives of the governor of the province; the Roman government, however, regarded this form of administration as transitional. As a result of the policy of urbanisation most of the non-urban territories were transformed into cities in the course of the second and third centuries. The exception was made in the areas of exceptional economic importance (such as the Jordan Valley estates). which the imperial treasury wanted to keep for itself. Also excepted were the regions whose inhabitants refused to conform to the prevailing pattern of Greco-Roman culture, which was regarded as a precondition of urban life. West of the Jordan only Upper Galilee remained in this latter category, because of the strength of its Jewish population there. In the lands beyond the river the non-urban areas included for the time being, most of Herod's

former possessions in Gaulanitis, Batanaea, Trochonitis and
Auranitis.[47]

This paragraph of Avi-Yonah's has been the inspiration for
much of this work. The cultural unity we have come to observe
in Upper Galilee and western Gaulanitis, therefore, is
representative of the strength of the Jewish population there
and not indicative of any sense of cultural or intellectual
deprivation. By this we do not mean sheer numbers—and we
do not think that Avi-Yonah meant this either; rather, we
mean that Jewish life in these isolated areas was vigorous and
healthy and basically aniconic, hardly to be described as
boorish, or the center of the 'am ha-aretz. The nonurbaniza-
tion of both Upper Galilee and western Gaulanitis may have
been therefore a reflection of the social and religious point of
view of the inhabitants.

It is important at this point to provide some additional data
on Upper Galilee. In our archaeological work at Khirbet
Shema', Meiron, and Gush Halav these past nine years, the
majority of city coins that have been retrieved from
excavation came from mints in the municipality of Tyre.[47a] The
importance of this fact cannot be overstated, for it shows that
the heartland of Upper Galilee was trading with and oriented
toward the Phoenician coast and not primarily with the Sea of
Galilee or Akko-Ptolemais. Indeed, the well-known story of
John of Gischala selling olive oil to his brethren in Tyre at a
substantial markup, enabling him to amass a great personal
fortune, seems to be an indication of the local economy. These
factors then urge us to use caution in assessing the isolation of
this region. Moreover, they enable us to explain many of the
cultural anomalies of the extreme north and may even help us
to place the northwestern boundaries of Galilee, or Tetracomia, in southern Lebanon.

When we speak of "villages" in Upper Galilee we are
speaking mainly about towns of approximately 30 to 50
dunams, such as Khirbet Shema'. Of all the Jewish sites in that

area, Meiron, at about 300 dunams, would appear to be the largest, if we include in it areas obscured by today's modern buildings along the southern extremity and Gush Halav, with its two synagogues and similar, perhaps larger, size. In western Golan a similar situation obtains in high-density areas of Jewish population. Qaysrein, around 120 dunams, is by far the largest site and like Meiron is linked to a whole string of settlements that cluster in the vicinity. No doubt there were good reasons for this pattern of settlement, having to do with agricultural systems, personal preference, safety, and the general desire of people to live among their own kind. We can therefore speak of a "network" of villages in both areas, sharing in many cases water supply, fields, trade interests, and the like.

In Upper Galilee, Avi-Yonah has noted a remarkable continuity in the population that gives no indication of having participated in the Bar Kokhba War of 132–35 c.e.[48] If this was the case, then as newcomers moved into the area the already established community would have exerted a strong influence upon the material culture as it developed in the years following such a population shift. This would explain, for example, why "northern" ceramic forms came to predominate early in the second century. Also, as we have already indicated, there is a serious methodological question as to the extent to which post-70 or post-135 conditions reflect earlier patterns of culture. The issue of continuity, therefore, is quite significant. Since the bulk of art, architecture, and epigraphy comes from the late periods, we shall have to be cautious in using any of it in our assessment of the first century.

The question of the founding of many of these settlements must for the meantime rest on the evidence from literary sources. Surface finds cannot provide sufficient data for such conclusions. The list of priestly courses, Josephus, and the rabbinic literature are the best guides to settlement in the absence of archaeological field reports. In both Tetracomia and western Gaulanitis, the major period of settlement would

46

seem to be the late Second Temple to the period of the Bar Kokhba.[49] Survey work in the Golan and recent work at Meiron, however, suggest an additional wave of population into the Golan in the late fourth century, probably during the reign of Constantine II, when excessive tax burdens made economic life in parts of Upper Galilee untenable.[50] Lower Galilee absorbed many new immigrants from the coastal plain area after the revolt of Gallus Caesar in 351.[51]

We have observed that while Josephus is reliable on many matters of geographical detail, he is not primarily concerned with presenting a precise topographic picture of the country. Just as ambiguities of purpose affect his presentation of certain aspects of the Roman Wars, so too are his notations on Galilean geography marred by inconsistencies or lack of clarity at many points. There is, however, one thing in his treatment of the people of Galilee that astonishes us: his presentation of them as deeply devoted to the Law in theory and practice, contrary to most popular conceptions of Galileans that we find in the rabbis or the New Testament. This observation lends even further credibility to the thesis herein advanced that the conservatism in art and language of Upper Galilee is indicative of a deeply set religious perspective which extends into western Gaulanitis.

3

The Context
of Early Christianity and
Palestinian Judaism

Since World War II we have witnessed a veritable explosion of archaeological data from the Holy Land. The result has been that the scholar of New Testament, early Christian origins, or rabbinic Judaism, already hard pressed to keep abreast of developments in the literature of the field, feels all the more unable to cope with so much new data. Hence it is not at all uncommon for scholars simply to ignore these developments as too much to accommodate.

But scholars in other disciplines not normally associated with archaeology are beginning to appreciate the depth that this data can bring. For example, in the United States an entire discipline called "historical archaeology" is beginning to fill the gaps in our knowledge of the past two hundred years through excavation. It is not beyond conception that the same phenomenon will begin to take shape in historical studies in the Ancient Near East for the periods in question.

We turn to recent archaeological data from the three localities of Jerusalem, Nazareth, and Capernaum in order to grasp the historical context of the emergence of rabbinic Judaism (see p. 49-61) and early Christianity apart from purely literary evidences. A sharpened understanding of the historical setting of these two movements from the point of view of archaeology may have some important implications.

Jerusalem

Jerusalem, of course, is the Holy City, the goal of the pilgrim, but in antiquity it was also the center of commerce, government,[1] and culture. It is no surprise, then, that a disproportionate amount of time, money, and energy should have been poured into digging up the past there. In fact, the number of excavations in the Holy City has increased dramatically in the past fifty years.[2] In the first half of the past hundred years, about a dozen excavators worked in Jerusalem. Lieutenant Charles Warren excavated around the Temple Mount from 1865 to 1870.[3] Captain Charles Wilson surveyed inside the Old City from 1867 to 1868.[4] For the next twenty-five years, about a dozen foreigners directed archaeological work in and around Jerusalem, concluding with R. Weill's discovery of the Theodotus inscription and of the city-wall fragments of the Ophel investigations.[5]

From Weill's time, (1913–14, 1923-24) to the present, however, more than twenty-five separate archaeological excavations took place within the walls of the Old City.[6] The most extensive one of these, directed by Dr. Benjamin Mazar south and west of the Temple Mount, concluded in 1977.[7] Dr. Nahman Avigad has meanwhile directed similar broad excavations in the Jewish Quarter, also within the walls of the Old City.[8] Most recently, Yigal Shiloh has launched a new investigation of the hill of Ophel.

What is it that we now know from excavation that we could not appreciate from reading Josephus, the New Testament, the Mishnah, the Palestinian Talmud, or Hellenistic Jewish sources? We can say that archaeology has provided us with concrete evidence of an impressive walled city dating from Hasmonaean times. As early as 1894, Bliss exposed the city wall south of the present Citadel and followed it around what is today Mount Zion, the southwestern hill. He was able to trace this wall 177 meters southward, following the work of H. Maudslay during the years 1894–97. The city wall included projecting towers and a defense fosse. Bliss also followed this wall to a tower and gate at the southwest section of the city where the wall continued due east to a corner with a gate near the Pool of Siloam.[9] In the past few years Israeli scholars have exposed earlier Hasmonaean foundations beneath these walls.[10]

Near Mount Zion, C. N. Johns excavated within the Citadel and found the Hasmonaean defense wall with two towers.[11] After the Hasmonaean period, Herod the Great built here the three towers of Phasael, Hippicus, and Mariamne. All three were part of Herod's palace. Strictly speaking, only Phasael was for defense. Yet the massive defense wall with its towers is a mute witness to the intensity of warfare in the second century B.C.E. It also gives us a valuable clue to the relative wealth of the nation that could afford to erect so heavy a defense work. For despite Herod's personal wealth, the earthquake of 31 B.C.E., and the extent of national expenditures on his building project, prosperity was relatively high during his reign.

Some think that this system included an inner wall that ran northeast from the southwestern corner of the city protecting the Upper City. The inner wall was evidently a second wall of defense in case the outer wall was breached. This wall also included a fosse which ran toward the Temple Mount. It was probably Alexander Yannai (Jannaeus, 103–76 B.C.E.), the ruler so addicted to war, who devoted substantial resources of the city to establishing the line of this wall.[12]

It was under Herod the Great, or more properly Herod the Elder,[13] that Jerusalem began to emerge as a showplace of the East. For example, he erected the three above-mentioned towers at the western approach to the city. The tower of Phasael still stands 20 meters high, measuring about 21.4 by 17 meters. This tower is a solid core of stone masonry that would be impervious to the battering ram.

But even more striking are the remains of the foundations of Herod's palace in the immediate area.[14] Evidently Herod had a platform erected for his palace about 60 meters wide (east to west) and about 300 to 350 meters long (the excavators are not definite about its length). This is a most impressive structure by any standard. The platform for the palace was built by creating a grid of supporting walls within which workers poured enormous quantities of fill. By this means Herod raised his palace visually, making it an even more imposing structure. It occupied an area of at least 13,000 square meters. If half that available space was used for walls, streets, and storage, then there would be available 9,000 square meters on the ground floor for people. If we allow 7 square meters of space per person in public buildings, then this palace could accommodate 1,300 people at any one time.

Is it possible to figure out the plan of the city in Herod's day? Though certain points in the answer to this question are still under discussion, particularly the vexing problem of the date and position of the northernmost, or Third Wall, of Jerusalem, we can deduce certain of its characteristics. Most recently John Wilkinson has made a compelling argument from archaeological evidence that the Herodian streets so far unearthed seem to follow a grid generally oriented on the cardinal points of the compass. This grid outlines blocks 300 by 225 Greek feet, or about 97 by 76 meters.[15] Therefore each block would be about four times the area of those at Chorazin and Capernaum in the *galil*. On the other hand, the latter are smaller townlets in the hinterland. The blocks at the ancient commercial city of Dura-Europos in modern Syria, which was destroyed in the mid-third century C.E., are closer in size to those from Jerusalem. For example, *insula* (block) L7, which contained the synagogue of the city, was about 78 by 43 meters, or about half the size of the putative blocks in Jerusalem.[16] Herod's Jerusalem, if Wilkinson is right, with wide, finely paved streets on a large, rectangular grid would give a favorable urban impression.

Estimates of ancient populations vary widely. Nevertheless, if we use a figure of about 400 to 500 people per 10,000 square meters (one hectare), the usual figure for ancient cities, we arrive at a population of from 37,000 to 44,000 for Jerusalem in the first century C.E.[17] Josephus mentions many more people than this visiting Jerusalem during high holy days, but he is likely to be referring to those who were encamped around the city as well as to those staying in inns and with relatives.

The most impressive single edifice in the city was the temple. Herod ensured that it would be the dominant feature of Jerusalem by providing it with a rectangular platform, in effect an artificial Mount Olympus. This platform is just short of a mile around, or a total of 1,561 meters.[18] The total area of this enclosure is 14.2 hectares. If half this space was used for buildings and architectural features, and was otherwise unavailable for standing, then the Temple Mount would comfortably hold a capacity crowd of about 75,000 people. This would have been easily exceeded at times of dense crowding, when the people might stand shoulder to shoulder.[19] Incidentally, the modern Western Wall (sometimes popularly called the Wailing Wall) represents only about 10 percent of the length of the exterior west side.

The entry to this enclosure was through the Huldah Gates in the south wall. The gates led to two ramps that sloped upward to the level of the interior. The interior height was at least 35 meters above bedrock in several places.[20] The ramp to the west is still to be seen. Its entry is today called the Double Gate, though it has been walled up perhaps since Umayyad times (ninth century C.E.). The Mishnah mentions that the Huldah Gates "served for coming in and for going out" (*Middot* 1.3), and that "whoever entered the Temple Mount came in on the right and went around and came out on the left" (2.2), which seems to mean that a person entered by one ramp and exited by the other.

At the top, south end of the Temple Mount, or Herod's enclosure, stood a long, colonnaded building called the Royal

Portico. Josephus is quite precise in describing this great structure. It stood on 162 columns, in four rows, its middle aisle stood over 30 meters high, and one must walk 13 meters to traverse the middle.[21] Colonnades stood on all four sides, but only this one is securely identified by Josephus. From the Book of Acts we might deduce that the eastern colonnade was called Solomon's Portico (3:11).

The temple proper, or sanctuary, was a priestly edifice and was therefore not open to ordinary lay people. Furthermore, the interior of the enclosure space was divided into progressively more exclusive spaces, or courts. The outermost court was for anyone, but Gentiles could go no farther. Josephus explains that a barrier (the *soreg* in Hebrew) three cubits in height (1.65 meters) separated this court from the court of Israel. He further asserts that it was pierced by thirteen gates, each of which bore an inscription in Latin and Greek that decreed death to Gentiles who should enter. One virtually intact example of this inscription has been found plus a fragment of another. Both are in Greek (see below, chapter 4).[22]

Since the site of the temple proper is now occupied by the Dome of the Rock, a structure held holy by Muslims, there has been no archaeological investigation of the Temple Mount proper in this century, nor is there likely to be. Investigations of the cisterns and other cavities beneath the Temple Mount in the last century brought many interesting water installations to light, not a few of which may have been passages and ritual baths from Herod's temple.[23]

Nevertheless, enough has been found south and west of the Temple Mount to suggest that certain ancient aphorisms are literally true. "Whoever has not seen Herod's building, has never seen anything beautiful" (b. *Baba Batra* 4a; b. *Ta'anit* 23a). The New Testament words "And . . . some spoke of the temple, how it was adorned with noble stones and offerings" is also called to mind (Luke 21:5).[24] Excavations at the south and west of the Temple Mount have given us many decorated architectural fragments that provide a clue to the richness of the building. These are floral and geometric designs on stucco and stone. In other words, Herod followed the injunction of the second commandment scrupulously, but his architects and craftsmen still managed to produce sumptuous and rich designs.[25]

As one approached from any direction the overall impression of the Temple Mount was one of grandeur. We can flesh out this statement in detail thanks to the most recent excavations. A street connected the western Upper City to the western side of the Mount via a great footbridge over what is called today Wilson's Arch, the only complete arch preserved on the western Mount. Another 6.4-meter-broad well-paved street ran south along the western wall and under the arch. Those walking there passed rows of shops that backed up to the great enclosure wall. Just north of the southeast corner, this street passed beneath another massive bridge, today's Robinson's Arch, which bore a wide street to a staircase that turned south.

Above the heads of pedestrians at this corner stood the corner tower, the cornerstone of which has been found. It was inscribed in Hebrew: "Belonging to the place of trumpeting." Here a priest blew blasts on the shofar to signal the beginning of Sabbaths and other holy days.[26] The paved street turned east at the southwest corner to hug the south wall of the temple enclosure. One walked to the east toward the monumental entry at the Huldah Gates on this street, which was sometimes stepped.

Near the Double Gate, archaeologists found the approach staircase to the southern entries of the Temple Mount. This was in the form of a 64-meter-broad staircase cut into bedrock and paved.[27] A wide, paved plaza filled out the area south of the broad stairway. Its eastern side was not found, but if it was roughly symmetrical it would have been about 166 meters east to west and have projected southward from the base of the stairway some 13 meters.

Other interesting features brought to light by archaeology include an underground passageway under what today is called the Triple Gate. It started 69 meters west of the southeast corner of the Temple Mount. This passage led 69 meters north to the series of vaulted arches holding up the area interior to the enclosure in the southeast (Solomon's Stables). Its builders carefully fitted blocks on masonry cut in Herodian style to form an underground hall 3.45 meters high by 1 meter wide.[28] The excavators have found various chambers cut into the bedrock at this southern entry. Some they interpret as ritual baths or *mikvaoth*. Others are simply cisterns or storage areas.

Many finds were scattered through the area south of the Temple Mount. These include fragments of the soft, white stoneware that is typical of the Herodian period. At least one is labeled in Hebrew *"qorban"* (sacrifice). Other discoveries include almost two thousand coins of the period, many stone weights (including some inscribed "loyal to Caesar"), and, of course, the ever-present pottery sherds.[29]

For all the magnificence and hauteur of this edifice, other finds in Jerusalem are suggestive of simpler, family living. The most fascinating is perhaps the house of the Bar Kathros family, found in the modern Jewish Quarter.[30] This house was destroyed in the general havoc wrought by the Romans in 70 C.E. The family here enjoyed six rooms and a bath with a living area downstairs of 55 square meters. A second story probably brought the total area to about 90 to 95 square meters. The size of the living area implies that a family of eight or nine members could live here comfortably by ancient standards. In its final destruction by fire, no one came back to disturb the remains. This bespeaks the urgency with which the inhabitants fled for their lives. One did not escape, however. The bones of the arm of a young woman were found in the ashes of the kitchen. They were leaning upright against the outer wall, resting with the palm on a step. This kitchen had been furnished with three clay and stone ovens, a round stone table, and a pair of heavy grinding stones. Other finds in the rest of the house included the usual pottery, pieces of furniture, coins, glass, stone cups, lids, and stoppers. A fine set of weights was marked "Of Bar Kathros" in Aramaic. This is the name of a prominent family mentioned in the Talmud (*Pesahim* 57a). The family had a poor reputation because of their practice of nepotism in temple appointments.[31]

Other finds in Jerusalem include the waterworks, the Antonia Fortress northwest of the Temple Mount,[32] remains of a possible shrine to Asclepius (the Greek god of healing and medicine) at the pool of Bethesda,[33] other pools, houses, and the great cemetery surrounding the city. Together they add up to a large, bustling city of cosmopolitan population.

Nazareth

Nazareth is not mentioned in ancient Jewish sources earlier than the third century c.e. This likely reflects its lack of prominence both in Galilee and in Judaea.[34] Archaeological investigations at Nazareth over the years have provided some important evidences for interpreting the nature of this Galilean locality.

Judging from the extent of its ancient tombs, Nazareth must have been about 40,000 square meters in extent, which corresponds to a population of roughly 1,600 to 2,000 people, or a small village. The finds of the Franciscan fathers, excavating here from 1955 to 1960, imply that the principal activity of these villagers was agriculture.[35] Nothing in the finds suggests wealth. Therefore Nazareth would have no particular claim to fame, which might illuminate the retort of Nathanael, "Can anything good come out of Nazareth?" (John 1:46). On the other hand, this small hamlet was not completely isolated. Josephus mentions Japha (or Yaphia), one and a half miles southwest of Nazareth, as one of the cities of Galilee that he fortified (*Wars* II.26.6). Yaphia is on the main Roman road that leads from Jerusalem north to Sepphoris, the capital of Lower Galilee. Nazareth was therefore close enough to lines of communication that news of the day would not bypass its residents.

The archaeological finds from this village go back as far as Abraham, or the Middle Bronze Age. Yet it is not clear that Nazareth was a settlement for more than a very few families from Middle Bronze I to Late Bronze II, or just before the entry of the Israelites into the land. It is in the second century B.C.E. that extensive remains are to be found, which suggests that this is the period of the refounding of the village. Pottery and other objects of all later periods are represented in the excavations.[36] This implies that the village was less than two hundred years old in the first century C.E., but that it continued to be attractive to settlers up to the present.

It is also clear from circumstantial evidence that Nazareth was a thoroughly Jewish settlement. It has been known for many years that Nazareth was one of the Galilean towns into which one of the twenty-four priestly courses resettled after the destruction of Jerusalem in 70 C.E. To be acceptable to priests it would have to be an unmixed city. A poem of Elkalir, usually dated to the sixth century C.E., mentions Nazareth in this connection.[37] Fragments of a list of the courses in Elkalir's order were found engraved on stone at Caesarea and at Ashkelon.[38] Nazareth is on the Caesarea fragment.

It is not possible to deduce the layout of the village from the remains so far excavated, nor is it possible to reconstruct the size and precise plan of any of its houses. Most probably, arguing from what is known about houses in other ancient villages, they were composed of small groups of rooms around a central courtyard. Some houses in Nazareth had two stories. Nazareth, then perched alongside the hill in a kind of basin some 345 meters above sea level, would not have been a particularly impressive sight. Its houses and public buildings were not more than one might see anywhere in Galilee.

Capernaum

Capernaum was the first town within Herod Antipas' realm as one comes from Bethsaida which lay within the tetrarchy of Philip. The name Capernaum is likely a corruption of the Hebrew *Kfar Nahum* ("the village of Nahum").[39] The Nahum in question is hardly the biblical prophet, but likely the otherwise-unknown original owner of the land. Capernaum was larger than Nazareth, stretching east to west along the northern coast of the Sea of Galilee. The Franciscans believe that the total size was about 500 by 200 meters.[40] Yet there is some evidence that the lake was higher in antiquity and that ruins extend under the modern level of the water. In fact, Wilson and Warren report that the ruins stretch one-half mile by one-fourth mile. The first area would be 100,000 square meters, while the second would be about 324,756 square meters. If we accept 300,000 square meters as approximately correct, the ancient population would have been between 12,000 and 15,000.[41] It should be no surprise that Capernaum is substantially larger than Nazareth, for it was the seat of a tax collector according to Mark 2:14. Avi-Yonah believes that the presence of this officer also implies that Capernaum was probably at the eastern extremity of Galilee.[42]

The town was laid out in regular blocks of one-story houses. Each block was about 40 by 40 meters, which is not large in comparison to Jerusalem. Such a block might contain three or four houses with common walls. Each house, as is likely at Nazareth, would contain a group of rooms around a central courtyard. Ovens and other domestic installations stood in the courtyards. Outside staircases led to flat roofs, for these were ideal working areas and doubled as sleeping places in the hot summer months. The walls were of unmortared black basalt, common to the region. The stones were cut roughly square and carefully stacked. Roofs were normally constructed of beams, branches, rushes, and mud. Such buildings have a high "heat mass" and would be relatively cool in summer and warm in winter. Windows were small and located high up for letting light in, not for seeing out.

Although the New Testament mentions a synagogue in Capernaum (Mark 1:21), no synagogue of the first century came to light in the modern excavations. The large fourth- and fifth-century synagogue excavated since 1914 was built not on top of an earlier synagogue but on houses.[43] Of course, it may be that the first-century house of prayer was a converted house, as was the case during the third century for the synagogue at Dura-Europos.

In any case, the excavators at Capernaum have found no public buildings of the first century. This does not mean that they do not exist, only that they have not yet been found. If anyone discovers a synagogue of the first century at Capernaum, it will most likely resemble the small synagogue at Magdala.[44] If we use this building as an analogue, we would expect the Capernaum edifice to be devoid of iconography, simple, with columns inside to hold up the roof. There would probably be benches on three sides, or perhaps on the wall opposite Jerusalem.

The pottery and other finds from this town indicate that its history, like Nazareth's, goes back to the second century B.C.E. The principal occupations of the inhabitants were probably agriculture and fishing, though trade was surely also important. A Roman milestone of the emperor Hadrian (117–138 C.E.) implies that a Roman road of the second century passed through here, probably following an already established route.[45]

We cannot leave Capernaum without mentioning the House of Saint Peter, found by the Franciscans.[46] Today the southernmost block of houses so far excavated at Capernaum (the *"insula sacra"* or Block I) is covered by an octagonal Byzantine church of the fourth and fifth centuries C.E. The singular shape of this church alerts us to expect a Christian holy place, or *loca sancta,* since it was the custom in the

Byzantine period to erect octagonal churches over places holy in Christian memory.[47]

The church in question was centered on one room of the block beneath. This room is 7.0 by 6.5 meters, large for an ancient house. (The synagogue at Magdala measures 8.17 by 7.25 meters.) The lowest floors of this room had early Roman pottery and coins sealed between them, which must mean that the founding and earliest use of this room, and therefore of the entire block of houses, was in the first century B.C.E. Either late in the first century or early in the second century C.E. this room received extensive interior remodeling: the floors were renewed several times and plastered, as were the walls. Sometime before the fourth century C.E. the pottery ceased to be simply domestic items. Ceramics discovered here dated after the first century tend to be storage jars and other "public" wares.[48]

The rough walls of this room received plaster three times in their history before the fourth century. One hundred thirty-one graffiti appeared on the plaster at the hands of pilgrims in the course of the years.[49] These were scratched in Greek, Aramaic, Syriac, and Latin. Those that can be reconstructed contain prayers to Jesus, and a few even mention the name of Peter, who lived in Capernaum, according to the Gospels (e.g., Mark 1:29). In the fourth century this room was enlarged, provided with an arch across the middle to hold up a heavier roof, plastered, and painted in designs. A large enclosure wall surrounded the whole. This is likely the church seen by Egeria in the late fourth century.[50]

Capernaum, therefore, a large town in the first century C.E., was important enough to be the residence of a regional tax collector. There are details of town planning which suggest a centralized government. Fishhooks from beneath the floors in one room confirm that fishing was surely one important activity in this town, as does the discovery of the remains of an ancient harbor.[51] Certainly agriculture and trade played a role in the local economy also.

Conclusions

From the evidence surveyed above, we get a bird's-eye view of three localities important in Jewish and Christian tradition. They provide us with a sketch of city, town, and village life in the first century. Jerusalem is obviously a grandly conceived center of national life, though it was no longer the capital after 6 C.E. Nazareth, at the opposite extreme, is a tiny agricultural hamlet somewhat off the main lines of communication but with fairly ready access to them. Capernaum, a regional center of some significance, strikes a middle ground between the two in terms of urbanism, city planning, wealth, and regional importance. Towns and cities such as these provided the living context within which the Jewish and Christian traditions played out their respective roles in history.

4

The Languages of Roman Palestine

One of the perennial problems in understanding the culture of Roman Palestine is how much and to what extent the Greek language was common. There is broad agreement among scholars that Aramaic was the dominant language of the people. There is also acknowledgment that Greek loomed large in commerce, government, and social interchange among the educated. There is less agreement, however, about the penetration of Greek into outlying areas, its use among less educated people, the everyday use of Hebrew, or the use of Hebrew by people who were not sages and scholars.

The historical situation is fairly well known. One of the first major historical events in Palestine that has linguistic implications is the deportation of Palestinian Jews to Babylon. In this case a captured, Hebrew-speaking people found themselves in an alien culture where the *lingua franca* was Aramaic, though other local languages were known. This marks the beginning of the earnest Aramaicization of the Hebrew language. (We must point out that Aramaic and Hebrew had already coexisted for some time, though not necessarily peacefully.)

A biblical incident illustrates this international bilingualism, at least on the part of the members of the ruling class in

Israel. In II Kings 18:19, Sennacherib, king of Assyria, sent his messenger Rabshakeh to King Hezekiah in Jerusalem, and a conversation in Hebrew took place between Rabshakeh of the Assyrians and Hezekiah's representatives. Eliakim ben Hilkiah, who was the king's steward, responded, "Pray, speak to [us] your servants in the Aramaic language [*aramît*], for we understand it; do not speak to us in the language of Judah [*yehudîth*] within the hearing of the people who are on the wall" (18:26). Rabshakeh was not to be persuaded, and he proceeded to shout in Hebrew (yehudîth, 18:28), evidently with the express purpose of rattling the guards standing on the wall!

This incident took place in the sixth century B.C.E. Hebrew had been in use as a written language at least since the twelfth century B.C.E., and the earliest known texts in Aramaic date perhaps as early as the late tenth or early ninth century B.C.E.[1] Therefore, the histories of the two languages overlap by several centuries.

Because of the ascendancy of Aramaic as the common language of the Near East from the Mediterranean to India (Pakistan), it seems to have been inevitable that Hebrew would gradually disappear as a broadly known tongue. With the emergence of the power of Assyria and Babylon, their common language, Aramaic, gradually gained in prestige and geographical dispersion. Indeed, it became the language of international correspondence, commerce, and trade from the Mediterranean to India and from Asia Minor to Egypt. In this linguistic situation it was also inevitable that Hebrew would be used less and less by fewer and fewer people. Hebrew became a minor, local language.

The return of the Jews to Palestine after the edict of Cyrus in 537 B.C.E. did little to change this linguistic picture. A possible allusion to the gradual loss of classical Hebrew by the Jews lies in Nehemiah 8, where the "book of the law of Moses" is read aloud to the people. Verse 8 explains, "And they read from the book, from the law of God, *mephorash;* and they gave the sense, so that the people understood the reading." What is

63

this word *mephorash?* The RSV renders it "clearly" but gives "with interpretation" in the margin. A similar word in Ezra 4:18 is rendered "plainly" in the RSV. But the context implies translation, as does the verse in Nehemiah. Although there is no clear consensus among scholars, there is reason to believe that for at least some citizens of Judaea translation would be necessary. Thus Jacob M. Meyers in the Anchor Bible translates the verse as follows: "They read from the book of the law of God in translation to make it intelligible and so helped them to understand the reading."[2]

The conquest of the Near East by Alexander the Great ushered in a new age. It is not that no one knew Greek in Palestine earlier than Alexander but that now it stood as a matter of governmental policy to use Greek in official transactions. Thus Greek quickly came to be the ordinary language of government, international relations, international trade, daily business, and conversation among the educated, though Aramaic continued to be used in literary as well as commercial circles.

The depth of penetration of Greek into ordinary life is debated, but an illustration of the early weight given to Greek is the production of the Septuagint, the translation of the Bible into Greek, about 275 B.C.E. After this time Jewish authors also composed certain books of the Apocrypha in Greek. These writings found their way into the Septuagint, as for example I and II Maccabees and The Wisdom of Solomon to name only three. This form of the Bible became standard text throughout the early Jewish Diaspora, or Dispersion (Hebrew: *galut*), and is the text often presupposed by the New Testament authors.

Hebrew and Aramaic did not disappear though, as witness the number of manuscripts in Aramaic from the Wadi Daliyeh (see below). Other writings in these two Semitic tongues were found near Qumran and are most commonly known as the Dead Sea Scrolls.[3] Though some have argued that these writings are evidence of a deliberate effort to revive a dead language, Hebrew, it is by far the consensus today that

Hebrew remained a live option for certain families who never lost command of their ancient tongue.

The Aramaic scrolls are largely translations *(targumim)* of biblical books, such as the Targum of Job and the Genesis Apocryphon (though the latter is really a free paraphrase and rewriting of Genesis). On the other hand, there are books that were clearly composed "from scratch" in Aramaic, such as the pseudo-Danielic fragments from Cave IV.

Therefore, although Greek was becoming the *lingua franca* of the whole Near East, Aramaic continued both as a literary language and as the household language of most Jews. Evidence for the latter are the many graffiti in Aramaic scrawled on stone ossuaries of the first centuries B.C.E. and C.E.[4] Ossuaries are short stone or wood boxes for reburial of the bones one year after primary inhumation in the family tomb (see chapter 5). Looking at the known figures concerning ossuary inscriptions, we find that out of a corpus of 194 inscribed ossuaries, 26 percent are inscribed in Hebrew or Aramaic, 9 percent are in Greek *and* a Semitic language, and 64 percent are inscribed in Greek alone.[5] This is important data for estimating the relative frequency of these three languages.

It was Pompey's march into Jerusalem in 63 B.C.E. that marked the advent of a new cultural dominance. The Roman province of Syria was established, and a new language was introduced. The Roman cultural, political, military, economic, and religious influence was there to stay. Yet Latin gained no firm foothold in the Near East, except in Roman military matters. After all, the Romans adored all things Greek and actively promoted the Hellenization of all their eastern territories. Therefore it is no surprise that Greek gained in use while Latin remained the language of narrow, specialist application.

The cultural weight of Rome remained the prominent feature in the Near East until the transition to the Byzantine Empire, usually dated to the Constantinian dynasty of the fourth century C.E. Yet Greek did not fade in favor of other languages, nor did Aramaic and Hebrew disappear. Rather, the linguistic situation remained at least stable, though other dialects of Aramaic (e.g., Nabataean and Syriac) gradually emerged, and non-Palestinian languages appeared with the bloom of Christian pilgrimages in the fourth century (e.g., Armenian and Georgian).

This rough historical outline of the major events bracketing linguistic shifts in Palestine can do no more than introduce the subject. Yet these events are crucial for understanding the emergence of the literatures of Judaism and Christianity in Palestine, and for understanding the development of the specific Palestinian dialects of these languages, to the extent that they can be identified. This history also has a bearing on the question of the language of the synagogue and the language of Jesus and the apostles, not to mention the question of the "original language" of the Gospels. Finally, language considerations come to bear also on questions of interpretation of intertestamental writings, the New Testament, and Mishnah and Midrash, not to mention Qumran.[6]

We now turn to a detailed discussion of the major languages of Palestine in the postbiblical period. For convenience we will start with Hebrew, followed by Aramaic, Greek, and Latin. We will mention a few other languages just to round out the picture.

Hebrew

Hebrew is the oldest language of the Bible and was probably the oldest language spoken at the turn of the first century C.E., since we may safely surmise that by this time Canaanite had disappeared. Inscriptional material for Hebrew exists from the twelfth century B.C.E., and perhaps earlier, if the Aphek ostracon (a text written in ink on a potsherd) can be dated earlier than first reports indicate.[7] There is no agreement about the relative ages of the Hebrew used in the Bible, but generally it is felt that most of what we read today was finally written down in the sixth century B.C.E., though much older forms of the language are preserved therein.

We have already mentioned the gradual displacement of Hebrew as a spoken language by Aramaic. While this is true, we must not assume that Hebrew always had to be learned as a dead tongue. Yet we have no hard evidence that Hebrew was the common language of people in Palestine between the period of Ezra and Herod the Great, even though many of the intertestamental books appeared first in Hebrew. In the Apocrypha, for example, we have the express notice by the grandson of Joshua ben Sira (Jesus the son of Sirach) that he translated his grandfather's book into Greek from Hebrew soon after 132 B.C.E. ("When I came to Egypt in the thirty-eighth year of the reign of Euergetes and stayed for some time. . . ."—from the prologue).[8] Several fragments of the Hebrew text of this book were found in 1952 in Cave II of Qumran and therefore are among the Dead Sea Scrolls. Other fragments were discovered at Masada.[9] It is likely that other books of the Apocrypha were also composed in Hebrew, although composition in Aramaic cannot be excluded.

The Dead Sea Scrolls themselves are far more often extant in Hebrew than Aramaic. How are we to explain this fact? The obvious answer is that the residents at Qumran read and wrote Hebrew. But does it follow that they also *spoke* Hebrew? Some of the scholars associated with the early research on the scrolls believed that this late Hebrew was the normal spoken dialect of the Jews in Judaea during this period. Others are of the opinion that Hebrew is only a second language learned by sages and scholars, much like Latin in the Middle Ages.[10]

The Copper Scroll from Cave II at Qumran is also in Hebrew. Its publisher dated it to the first half of the second century C.E.[11] This document is sometimes called a treasure scroll, since it contains what purports to be hiding sites of the Temple treasure. But for our purposes it is important that it was written in Hebrew. Presumably it was intended to be a permanent record that only a Jew could read, in fact, perhaps only a member of a priestly, or rabbinic, family.

Ossuary inscriptions in Hebrew are also well known. That

any of them are in Hebrew is highly significant. Surely these simple graffiti, usually recording only the name of the person whose bones are housed therein, are intended for the family of the deceased.[12] Two ossuary lids from Bethphage, just east of Jerusalem, are of special importance here.[13] One, for example, contains twenty-seven Hebrew names, such as Ben Hasir, Ben Tehinna, Ben Hadda, Ben Joseph Nazir, Ha-Gelili, Ben Azaria, and so on. Each name is followed by numbers in the Nabataean script. Some scholars identify these as paylists of an undertaker's employees, though others interpret the list as a roster of those who have died and the dates of their deaths. In either case, we have Hebrew names, though the Nabataean numbers are a surprise. It may suggest that the head undertaker was from Transjordan, though the Nabataeans lived also in the eastern Negev at this time.

The ossuaries from Dominus Flevit, which is located on the Mount of Olives in Jerusalem, to name just one other site of important finds, are also instructive in this regard.[14] Besides the usual names, we also have other Hebrew words. For example, number 39 reads "Martha, our mother" in Hebrew. Number 31 carries the Hebrew inscription "Salome, the proselyte." Number 12 names the vocation of the deceased: "John, the craftsman," also in Hebrew. Another set of Hebrew ossuary inscriptions comes from Jerusalem on Mount Scopus.[15] In a burial vault of four chambers with many ossuaries and sarcophagi, one Hebrew inscription reads "Hanania, son of Jonathan the Nazarite." Another ossuary in the same chamber contains the Hebrew phrase "Salome wife of Hanania, son of the Nazarite."

We pointed out above that these inscriptions are intended for the family. This may likely mean that the family used Hebrew as a matter of course. No doubt these are likely to be middle-class families, but that must not prevent us from noticing that Hebrew was a language of daily communication. The fact that it is used in the context of reburial in an ossuary also shows that this context was sacred, or holy.

Public inscriptions in Hebrew are also known in Jerusalem from the first half of the first century c.e. The most famous is that of the Tomb of James in the Kidron Valley just east of the Temple Mount.[16] Just above the two columns of the facade of this tomb, one sees an inscription in square Hebrew letters that reads: "This is the tomb and the memorial of Eleazar, Haniah, Joazar, Jehudah, Shimeon, Johannan, the sons of Joseph son of Obed [and also] of Joseph and Eleazar [the] sons of Haniah, priests [of the family] of the sons of Hezir."

The recent excavations at the Temple Mount in Jerusalem have turned up a fragment of a monument inscription in archaic Paleo-Hebrew letters. Unfortunately it is too fragmentary to read, but it is in two lines with dots as word dividers. The mason cut it into a fine white marble plaque 2.5 centimeters thick.[17] Of more interest is the inscription "Belonging to the place of trumpeting . . ." found at the southwest corner of the great temple enclosure.[18] This was surely the topstone of the southwestern tower, where a priest blew the shofar to usher in the Sabbath. Such inscriptions are intended to be read, that is, they reflect language habits of at least some of the people.

The Hebrew finds from Masada are especially helpful in this regard, for they can be dated to 68–73 c.e., or the exact period of the First Jewish Revolt.[19] They were intended for use by the Jewish defenders of that almost inaccessible fortress.

Documents in Hebrew include fragments of biblical books: Psalms, Leviticus, and Genesis. In addition, excavators found fragments of books of the Apocrypha and other sectarian literature, though their titles are not all known. Perhaps the greatest surprise in terms of manuscripts were the twenty-six fragments of the scroll of Ben Sira, or Ecclesiasticus.[20] They represent the original text of that book (though, to be sure, not the autograph scroll), which is otherwise represented in the Apocrypha in Greek and previously known from a fragmentary medieval Hebrew version.

Vessels bear names of their owners. They are often in Hebrew and in ink or charcoal. Certain storage jars and wine or oil amphoras were marked with a Hebrew letter, a *tav,* which appears to have been an abbreviation for the Hebrew word *terumah,* or "offering." The excavators found several "tags" with Hebrew letters on them, evidently also abbreviations. One of the tags found in the synagogue read, in Hebrew, "priest's tithe" in cursive script.

Such finds are particularly important, for they can be dated to a narrow range of years. They also suggest that Hebrew tended to be used for activities associated with the cult: scrolls, the offering, priestly tithe, and so on. But the fact that Hebrew names appear to mark ownership makes the use of Hebrew seem less sacerdotal and more nationalistic in this context. Thus, although the evidence for spoken Hebrew is not abundant, there is enough data to suggest that some families used Hebrew in intrafamilial discourse in the first centuries B.C.E. and C.E..

Yet the Bar Kokhba archive found in the Wadi Muraba 'at and the Wadi Habra in the Judaean desert[21] clearly indicates that Hebrew survived the first century. This archive throws sudden and resplendent light upon an obscure but important facet of Jewish history. Scholars knew from ancient literary sources that a revolt of the Jews against the Romans had been led by a certain Bar Kokhba, which means "son of a star," but it was not even clear that this was his correct name. Part of the historical difficulty has also been that Christian sources preserve this name, whereas the brief ancient Jewish sources called him "Bar Koziba" ("son of a liar"). Further complicating the record is evidence that Rabbi Akiba of the second century C.E. actually went so far as to say, "This is the King Messiah," though his friend and colleague Rabbi Johannan bar Tortha retorted, "Akiba, grass will grow in your cheekbones and he still will not have come!" (*b. Gittin* 57-58).

Coins from this period are abundant indeed.[22] Often they are Roman coins overstruck with the legend and designs of the

Second Revolt. The inscriptions are in Hebrew, and they read "Year One of the Redemption of Israel," "Year Two of the Freedom of Israel," or "of the Freedom of Jerusalem." The latter inscription gives no year. Thus the coins seem to indicate that there was a real revolt, but the name of the leader of the revolt was not included in the coin legend.

The entire story changed in October 1951, when some Bedouins of the Ta'amireh tribe (famous for their accidental discovery of the Dead Sea Caves and the scrolls) brought into the Palestine Archaeological Museum (now the Rockefeller) fragments of parchment scrolls in Greek and Hebrew. They divulged the source as a large cave in the Wadi Muraba 'at about three kilometers west of the Dead Sea. The story is much longer, but our interest lies in the major expedition launched by the Israelis beginning in 1953.

In the so-called Cave of Letters these explorers found a bundle of papyrus documents tied in antiquity with string. There were also wooden slats with Aramaic writing in ink. Each papyrus was neatly folded as though for storage. This bundle, and another bundle found at the Wadi Muraba 'at, to the north, contained letters in Aramaic, Greek, and Hebrew dictated by Shimeon ben Kosiba (Bar Kokhba) to his field commanders at En-gedi. The Hebrew letter in the first cache may even be in Bar Kokhba's own hand. It reads:

> From Shimeon ben Kosiba to Jeshua
> ben Galgoula and to the men of the fort,
> Shalom. I take heaven to witness against me
> that unless you mobilize [destroy?] the Galileans
> who are with you,
> every man, I will put fetters
> on your feet as I did
> Ben Aphlul.[23]

Among the Wadi Muraba 'at discoveries were four letters, two of which were in Hebrew and also sent to Jeshua ben Galgoula. These evidently stemmed from Jeshua's own archive. In addition to these documents a second cache of papyri from the Cave of Letters consisted of deeds, four in Hebrew and two in Aramaic. The total set of manuscripts also included biblical fragments in Hebrew. This is no surprise, considering the wealth of such fragments from Qumran. But what is more pertinent for understanding the spoken languages of Palestine in the second century C.E. are the number of other documents in Hebrew. These include, besides a phylactery, a hymn or prayer from a burial, two bills of divorce, and a marriage contract, also five real estate transactions, twelve contracts concerning rental of fields nationalized by Bar Kokhba and guaranteed by his authority, and of course the letters.

Yet another linguistic phenomenon occurring exactly at the beginning of the third century C.E. dramatizes perhaps even more clearly the position of Hebrew as the language of the scholarly community. This is the compilation of the Mishnah by Judah ha-Nasi ("the Prince," also called in the tradition simply "Rabbi," with no qualifier).[24] The Mishnah is a compilation of a living Hebrew language tradition concerning the Law and its current application to life. For our purposes the interesting point is that it is in Hebrew, with a few exceptions in Aramaic (about fifteen paragraphs). The remainder of almost eight hundred pages in Danby's English edition is translated from Hebrew, but with many words borrowed from Aramaic, Greek, and even Latin.

In this regard it is interesting to read what this tradition says about Hebrew, or "the holy language." First we notice that the Mishnah simply assumed that a bill of divorce would be written in Hebrew or Greek, and that there might therefore be a problem if the witness signed in the other language (for then their names might not appear directly under their column): "If a bill of divorce was written in Hebrew and the names of the witnesses in Greek, or if it was written in Greek and the names of the witness in Hebrew . . ." (*Gittin* 9.8). "Hebrew" here may mean either Hebrew or Aramaic.

"The holy language" appears in several texts in the Mishnah. This suggests that biblical Hebrew was already recognizably different from Mishnaic, or current, spoken Hebrew. For example, the tractate *Sota* ("The Suspected Adulteress") contains a discussion of which cultic recitations may be given in "the holy language" (Hebrew) and which in "any language." What goes into which list is not so much germane here as the very fact that this was an issue. Clearly in this context "the holy language" must mean classical Hebrew, as biblical texts were to be recited. Thus, other languages are impinging on the domain once controlled by the classical language.

Therefore, the combined witness of the Mishnah and the Bar Kokhba discoveries suggests that Mishnaic Hebrew was a spoken language but that the classical language was preferred for certain cultic acts. That it was necessary to legislate which recitations could take place in "the holy language" indicates that someone was not doing things properly; otherwise, there would be no debate. Further evidence that we are dealing with spoken languages in Hebrew, and not merely literary languages, is afforded by the influence of Aramaic upon the vocabulary and syntax of this Mishnaic Hebrew. The peculiarities in spelling reveal that often Hebrew pronunciation is being recorded, a feature of a living language.

Aramaic

Scholars have agreed for many years that Aramaic was the dominant language of Palestine for the majority of its Jewish inhabitants. After all, the authors of Daniel and Ezra composed roughly half these books in Aramaic, a testimony to the strong position of this language after 400 B.C.E. But an earlier archaeological witness to the importance of Aramaic in early rabbinic Judaism is given by the discoveries at a cave in the Wadi Daliyeh.[25]

This cave opens some sixty meters back into a hill and was the last refuge for some important families from Samaria just before the conquest of Alexander the Great. Evidently refugees had occupied the cave in question just prior to the coming of Alexander to the Middle East. These people were wealthy Samaritans who had fled Alexander's advance, perhaps at his return from Egypt to put down a revolt of the Samaritans. Their enemies overtook them in their refuge and slaughtered them to the last man, woman, and child.

The papyri found in the cave seem to have been very important to these refugees. They were almost all legal or administrative in nature and they were in Aramaic. All were written in the province and/or city of Samaria. Many of the names preserved in them are Yahwistic (they contain element *"iah"* [*Yhwh*] at the end or *"Je"* [*Yhwh*] at the beginning). It is significant for understanding the languages of Palestine that these papyri appear in Aramaic, not Hebrew. Nevertheless, one seal is inscribed in a Paleo-Hebrew script and in the Hebrew language. It reads, "yahu, son of [San] ballat, governor of Samaria." We see that Hebrew still functions as a minor public, or official, language but that Aramaic is by far the dominant tongue.

Recent discoveries of mainly Aramaic ostraca from the south of Palestine at Khirbet el-Kôm (the ancient name of which is not known) from the early third century B.C.E. further document the extent of use of Aramaic.[26] The ostraca in question number five in Aramaic, one in Greek, and one in Aramaic and Greek. They all appear to be receipts of a moneylender named Qosyada (Koside), a certain Idumaean, and his fellow Idumaean, Qosbana. Ostracon 2 reads as follows:

> Qosyada to Jaaphat:
> two quarter-shekels.
> Qosbana to Malha: one shekel and
> two quarter-shekels.

One of these ostraca is dated "Year 6," which presumably means the sixth year of Ptolemy II Philadelphus, which corresponds to the year 277 B.C.E. in the Julian calendar. Ostracon 3 is dated 25 July 277 B.C.E.

What is significant here is that ordinary moneylending transactions were kept recorded in Aramaic and occasionally in Greek. Therefore in Idumaea, about thirty-six kilometers as the crow flies due southwest of Jerusalem, a small community between Hebron and Lachish, Aramaic was the main language of business.

Yet it is the great library of Qumran that provides us with most of the manuscripts composed or translated into Aramaic. For example, the Genesis Apocryphon is an extended collection of stories paraphrased from the patriarchal narratives in Genesis. It was written in Aramaic at the end of the first century B.C.E. or in the first century C.E. Likewise the Targum (translation) of Job is dated to the first century C.E. on the basis of its linguistic development and some internal evidence. Fragments of other works in Aramaic are also known from the caves: The Prayer of Nabonidus, The Testament of the Twelve Patriarchs, The Description of the New Jerusalem, Fragments of Enoch, etc. Though these are in the minority at Qumran, they tell us that Aramaic was definitely a literary language.

But it is also the ossuary inscriptions discussed above that lend us more understanding of Aramaic as a colloquial language. Some of these graffiti are important not only for the historical data they give us but also for the linguistic evidences. For example, at Giv'at ha-Mivtar in north Jerusalem, workmen discovered four Jewish tombs by accident in June 1968.[27] The ossuaries featured many Aramaic inscriptions, such as Ossuary 1 of Tomb 1, which reads, "Simon the Temple Builder." It appears that this Simon was one of the master masons or contractors who participated in building Herod's temple of Jerusalem. Ossuary 2 of that tomb reads, "Jehonathan the potter" in Aramaic. "Jehonathan" is a long form of "Jonathan." Ossuary 14, on the other hand, has a rather long two-lined inscription in Aramaic scratched in an unpracticed hand and therefore is difficult to decipher. It seems most reasonable to read: "This is the ossuary of Salome the daughter of Saul, who died in childbirth. Salome his daughter." The ossuary contained the bones of a woman thirty to thirty-five years old with a fetus at term, which tends to support the reading of the inscription.

Among the ossuaries of Dominus Flevit, of which one hundred twenty-two were recovered, seven were inscribed in Hebrew, eleven in Aramaic, and eleven in Greek.[28] This count includes one in Aramaic *and* Hebrew, and one other in Semitic and Greek ("Semitic" because it is impossible to distinguish whether it is Hebrew or Aramaic). Ossuary 32 reads simply, "Maria the daughter of Agra." Likewise, Ossuary 3 contained the reburial of a woman: "Salome the wife of Shapir."

Other ossuary or tomb inscriptions from the first century, also in Aramaic, are somewhat longer. For example, the tomb cave in the Wadi Salah of the Kidron Valley contains an inscription scratched above one of the burial slots: "This burial slot has been made for the bones of our fathers; it is two cubits long, and do not open it."[29] Perhaps even more interesting is the inscription in Aramaic on an ossuary lid from the tomb of Jebel Khalet et-Thuri, south of the village of Siloam, which itself lies immediately south of Jerusalem: "Whatever a man may find for his benefit in this ossuary is an offering to God from him who is within it."[30]

One of the longest and most puzzling Aramaic tomb inscriptions is the so-called "Abba" inscription from Giv 'at ha-Mivtar.[31] Although the language is definitely Aramaic, the script is archaic Paleo-Hebrew, or old letters (but not the Babylonian square letters). It is carefully carved into the tomb wall:

> I, Abba, son of the priest Eleaz[ar],
> son of Aaron the high [priest], I
> Abba, the oppressed and the persecuted,

who was born in Jerusalem,
and went into exile in Babylon and
brought back [to Jerusalem] Mattathiah
son of Juda, and I buried him in the cave,
which I acquired by the writ.

It is possible that the use of the archaic Hebrew script at least reveals that its author is not a Pharisee, for the Pharisees preferred the square script. Abba's language, in any case, is Aramaic, and he expects his readers to be able to use it.

There also exists an Aramaic contract, or IOU, from Wadi Muraba 'at dated the second year of the reign of Nero, 56 C.E.[32] Likewise, from Masada comes an Aramaic invoice, an ostracon in two lines that demanded a payment of five hundred denarii.[33] A text written on a vessel identified the owner: "The High Priest Akbiah." In another part of the fortress, between two storerooms in the northeast, a jar featured an Aramaic inscription of several lines, the opening line of which says, "Offer[ing . . . of your bro]ther Jeho-hanan, Peace." These materials from Masada are especially important, for they reveal quite clearly that Aramaic appeared even on the most humdrum items, things far removed from romance and adventure.

We have already mentioned the Bar Kokhba archive in connection with the use of Hebrew in the land. Yet Aramaic is by far the most popular language of the letters.[34] For example, the first bundle of letters contained six in Aramaic, two in Greek, and one in Hebrew. Most of the Aramaic letters, like the Hebrew ones, were written to Jonathan ben Beaya and to Masabala bar Shimeon at En-gedi. The second cache found in the Bar Kokhba caves included four Hebrew deeds, two Aramaic deeds, and fifteen Greek papyri.

Here we should also mention the archive of Babata, daughter of Shimeon bar Menachem.[35] This was by far the largest bundle of manuscripts found in the Cave of Letters and it included thirty-five documents, of which three were in

Aramaic, twenty-six in Greek, and six in Nabataean, a dialect of Aramaic spoken in the kingdom of the Nabataeans south and east of the Dead Sea. That some of the documents are in Nabataean is explained by this lady's history, for she was originally from Mahoza in Nabataea. It is therefore all the more striking that none of her file is in Hebrew, although she is Jewish. One of the Aramaic documents is a deed for a palm grove. The deed is dated 18 December 99 C.E. The second Aramaic document is the marriage contract (*kethuba*) of Babata and Judah bar Eleazar of En-gedi, her second husband. It seems clear that the common languge of these people is Aramaic.

Probably during the course of the first century C.E. Targums (Aramaic translations of the Bible) were being written down for the first time. Evidence for this includes the Targum of Job from the Qumran cave and the Targum on Leviticus from the same cave. However, it seems that the most abundant texts of Targums date after 200 C.E., or after the compilation of the Mishnah.

The evidence seems overwhelming, then, that Aramaic was far more widely used in Palestine than Hebrew, although it did not reach the breadth of the use of Greek.

Greek

Many scholars have pointed out frequently that Greek culture was making inroads into Palestine long before the conquests of Alexander the Great.[36] For example, Greek pottery of the sixth century B.C.E. is known from various coastal sites in the country. Greek coins and their local Palestinian imitations are a staple before the fourth century B.C.E. The so-called proto-Ionic or proto-Aeolic capitals for pillars in buildings are known from as early as the Iron Age in Palestine. Yet our earliest dated Greek document in the land is to be found among the ostraca from Khirbet el-Kôm.[37]

Again we are speaking of eight ostraca, six in Aramaic, one

in Greek *and* Aramaic, and one in Greek. The bilingual one is especially interesting:

Aramaic text:	On the 12th of Tammuz, Year 6 Qosyada son of Hanna, the moneylender, loaned to Nikeratos: zûz 32.
Greek text	Year 6, 12th [day], month of Panemos, Ni- keratos, son of Sobbathos, received from Koside, the money- lender: 32 drachma.

The date corresponds to 25 July 277 B.C.E. Apparently, in the small town of Idumaea a man with a Greek name (Nikeratos), whose father has a Semitic name (Sobbathos), borrowed 32 drachmas (*zûz* in Aramaic) from Qosyada the moneylender. The word *moneylender* in the Aramaic text is actually a Greek loanword, *kapelos*. It is evidently a technical term and therefore borrowed directly.

Ostracon 6 appears to be in the hand of the borrower:

> I, Pestaus,
> the son of Domos, have from
> Qosyada the son of Ana [Hanana]
> 35 drachmas.

The name of Pestaus may be of Egyptian origin. In fact, the names of Qosyada's clientele are remarkably diverse. Names of Nabataean, Aramaean, Jewish, Greek, Arab, and Egyptian origins can be found. Clearly, then, these diverse ethnic elements required a common language. At this period Aramaic is the first choice, though Pestaus writes his receipt in Greek. It is not an elegant Greek, but it serves a business purpose.

The earliest other evidences for the presence of Greek in Palestine are inscriptions. The first group is political and public in nature. For example, from Joppa comes an inscription dated 217 B.C.E. erected in honor of Ptolemy IV Philopator of Egypt after his victory over Antiochus III of Seleucia.[38] From Hefzibah in Scythopolis (Beth Shean) comes a long inscription containing memoranda of two kings of Seleucia: Antiochus III (223–187 B.C.E.) and his successor Seleucus IV Philopator (187–175 B.C.E.).[39] An inscription from Akko-Ptolemais honors the later Seleucid ruler Antiochus VII Sidetes (138–129 B.C.E.) and his consort Cleopatra Thea.[40] This text is dated 130 B.C.E. and is also evidence of the ruler cult in that city.

The decree of Antiochus III from Hefzibah is too long to reproduce here *in extenso,* but we give some of it to show the assumptions made about public decrees:

> King Antiochus to Ptolemais, greetings . . . us [?], do order that, having inscribed on stelae of stone or white tablets [?] the letters, one shall set them up in the pertaining villages. We have also written about these matters to Cleon and Heliodoros the *dioketai* in order that they may act accordingly. Year 112, [month of] Hyperberetaios [September 200 B.C.E.] . . .

The word in italics is Greek for an official. Note that this is a public decree and that presumably at least some of the villagers would be able to read it.

Other Greek inscriptions reveal the extent of Greek religious institutions in Palestine or of other foreign religions in Greek dress. For example, at Ptolemais someone erected a Greek inscription dedicated to Zeus-Soter in 130 B.C.E.[41] Another from that same city and same century B.C.E. celebrated the names of Hadad and Atargatis.[42] From Samaria comes a Greek dedication to Serapis and Isis dated 201 B.C.E.[43] Another of the second century B.C.E. lists the priests of Zeus Olympius in Samaria.[44] From the first century B.C.E. we have graffiti from Eleutheropolis (biblical Maresha),[45] a statue from Bashan dedicated to Herod the Greek and dated 23 B.C.E.,[46] the Jason tomb in Jerusalem and its Greek graffito

("Rejoice, O living, and for the rest, drink and eat"),[47] and others.

But it is the apocrypha and pseudepigrapha that give us the largest corpus of Greek literature from Palestine in the last two centuries B.C.E. and the first century C.E.[48] This literature is fascinating in its own right and worthy of separate treatment. Let it suffice to point out here that the additions to the biblical books of Daniel and Esther, themselves composed in Hebrew and Aramaic, appeared now in Greek. That is, the Jewish authors of these additions appeared to believe that Greek was the proper language of literature.

It is also during this period that Jewish authors composed many examples of literature in Greek. Many of these works have not survived except to the extent that later Greek authors (such as Eusebius of Casearea or Clement of Alexandria) quoted them. However we do have the complete works of Flavius Josephus: *The Antiquities of the Jews, The Jewish Wars, Against Apion, Life,* and *Discourse to the Greeks Concerning Hades.*[49] Josephus bitterly attacks an opponent of his, also a Jewish historian, whose command of Greek may have exceeded that of Josephus himself. This is Justus of Tiberius, who even served as the emperor Vespasian's secretary.[50]

The explosion of Greek Palestinian literature has sometimes been taken as evidence that Greek was the language of the region. But we have already noted ample evidence for Aramaic and Hebrew during this period.

In order to document most accurately the language of the people, however, we are obliged to turn from literature to the ossuaries we considered before. In fact, it is well to remember that almost two-thirds of these inscriptions are in Greek. For example, an ossuary from a tomb-cave in the Kidron Valley of Jerusalem reads: "Thaliarchos, 20 years old. Thaliarchos son of Dositheos, 20 years old."[51] Another famous inscription recorded: "This is the ossuary of the Sons of Nicanor of Alexandria, who made the gates." In the case of the sons of

Nicanor, one might argue that the family used Greek because they were from Alexandria. But Thaliarchos the son of Dositheos was presumably a native of Jerusalem. Both he and his father used good Greek names. Incidentally, Nicanor and his donation of the temple doors are known also from ancient Jewish sources.[52]

Other items of information also appear in these Greek scratchings. For example, on Ossuary 21 from Dominus Flevit we read: "Diogenes the son of Zena, the proselyte." It was written twice. Ossuary 41 from the same site reads: "Mara, Storge, Chresimos the father of Demarchia." More often than not one reads simply the names of the deceased. Yet these prove beyond any reasonable doubt that the majority of Jewish families could read and write Greek and did so even for strictly family business.

Three inscriptions from the first century B.C.E., demonstrate again the pervasiveness of Greek in the land. The first is from Jerusalem and from Herod's temple. It is a limestone plaque announcing to Gentiles that entry to the inner courts of the temple is forbidden them: "No Gentile shall enter inward of the partition and barrier surrounding the Temple, and whoever is caught shall be himself responsible for his death which will follow."[53] The Greek word for Gentile used here is the same as that used by Josephus when he mentions that such inscriptions in Greek and Latin announced to non-Jews the limits of their access:

> When one goes through these first cloisters into the second court of the temple, there was a partition made of stone all around, whose height was three cubits. Its construction was very elegant. Upon it stood pillars at equal distances from one another, declaring the law of purity, some in Greek and some in Roman letters, that no Gentile should go within that sanctuary. [War 5.5.2]

That these inscriptions should be in Greek and Latin is of no surprise, since they are addressed to non-Jews. The second one is a surprise in several ways. This inscription has been known since 1914, when it was found in the course of the Ophel investigations in Jerusalem. During the first century C.E. someone hid it along with many fragments of a building, all neatly stacked together. It appears that the building had been destroyed (by Titus in 70? C.E.). Someone had carefully gathered some of its important architectural fragments and stored them in an unused cistern. The intent may have been to return and repair or reerect the building at a later date.

> Theodotos son of Vettenos, priest and Head of the synagogue, son of the Head of the synagogue, who was also the son of the Head of the synagogue, built the synagogue for the reading of the law and for the study of the commandments, as well as the hospice and the chambers and the bathing establishment, for lodging those who need them from abroad. It was founded by his ancestors and the elders and Simonides.[54]

For obvious reasons this has been called the "Theodotos inscription." It is interesting that his title is "Head of the synagogue" *(arche synagogos),* which is otherwise a title attested primarily in the New Testament. Futhermore, Theodotos is a third-generation head of a synagogue.

It is quite clear from this inscription that there are people of the first century in Jerusalem who can read and appreciate public announcements in Greek. It is interesting that the inscription announced the associated school ("the study of the commandments" in the text) in Greek, even though it appears that only study of the Torah was allowed in Jewish schools.

The third text is more difficult to date. It was found in Nazareth, if that is what its inventory notice means in the Cabinet des Medailles in Paris ("envoyée de Nazareth en 1878"). Some believe it is a genuine decree of Caesar, but which one? Scholars have proposed Augustus, Claudius, Tiberius, and even Hadrian. But the form of the letters appears to date their cutting to the first half of the first century, which would exclude Hadrian. Furthermore, Galilee did not come directly under imperial rule until the death of King Herod Agrippa in 44 C.E., which would suggest that we look to Claudius or Tiberius as the emperor under discussion. All this presupposes, of course, that the inscription actually is originally from Nazareth.

The text is in twenty-two lines on white marble 60 centimeters high by 37.5 centimeters wide. It is in Greek, but it seems to have been composed originally in Latin:

Decree of Caesar

It is my pleasure that sepulchres and tombs, which have been erected as solemn memorials of ancestors or children or relatives, shall remain undisturbed in perpetuity. If it be shown that anyone has either destroyed them or otherwise thrown out the bodies which have been buried there or removed them with malicious intent to another place, thus committing a crime against those buried there, or removed the headstones or other stones, I command that against such person the same sentence be passed in respect of solemn memorials of men as is laid down in respect of the gods. Much rather must one pay respect to those who are buried. Let no one disturb them on any account. Otherwise it is my will that capital sentence be passed upon such person for the crime of tomb-spoliation.[55]

Some have maintained that this is an ancient forgery. Whatever the case, the fact remains that it is in Greek. Presumably at least some of the local citizens were expected to read it.

The use of Greek extends into the second century, C.E., where the evidence from inscriptions is more abundant. In particular, we direct our attention to Beth She' arim in western Lower Galilee, the great necropolis and town that was the home of Judah ha-Nasi for so long.[56]

The ancient town of Beth She' arim was excavated beginning in 1936. Its most stunning feature is a set of catacombs and tombs dating from the first to the sixth century C.E. Since this was a Jewish town, we have invaluable historical, archaeological, and epigraphic information for reconstructing life in western Galilee. But many of the people buried in its necropolis were from the Diaspora, which attests to its status as a center for reburial.

According to the excavators, Catacombs 6, 11, 14, 20, 21, 22, and 23 belong to the earliest periods at Beth She' arim. Catacombs 6 and 11 may be of the late first or second century C.E., while the others are of the second and third centuries C.E. The epitaphs in Catacombs 6 and 11 are all in Greek. In the first catacomb only four letters of a name survive. But Catacomb 11 furnishes us with ample evidence for the use of Greek in this Galilean village. In Room I a certain Theodotus and his wife are buried:

> I, Theodotus, lie here
> together with Tatē.

Nearby in Room V a set of other epitaphs is preserved:

> I, Hesychios, lie here with my wife.
> May anyone who dares to open [the grave]
> above us not have a portion in the eternal
> life.

It is interesting to read the second sentence with its curse. Such burial curses are common at Beth She' arim and other sites. It is doubly interesting that "eternal life" is mentioned and not resurrection.

Another epitaph in Room V is signed by its authors:

> May your portion be good, my lord father
> with my lady mother, and may our souls
> belong to immortal life. Iako and Thino
> of ours [of our family?].

Iako (or Jako) and Thino may be brother and sister or Thino may be Iako's wife. Also carved into the wall of Room V is an inscription at the hand of a devoted nephew:

> This grave is one of the lowest coffins of all. And it is a good thing that it has been placed high, for it is my Uncle Papos, who brought us up.

It appears that this nephew visited the tomb and had to move ossuaries around to find the bones of his uncle so he moved the stone receptacle high on the pile. Presumably he felt it was the least he could do for the man who had reared him and his siblings.

Catacomb 20 has elicited considerable discussion as the possible burial place of Judah ha-Nasi and his relatives in the rabbinate. This is because, unlike the other catacombs at this site, the chambers of Catacomb 20 contained more Hebrew inscriptions than Greek. Also, the men all bear biblical names (though the women have Greco-Roman names).

Be that as it may, the Greek used is certainly a colloquial Greek, which makes it highly likely that Greek was their normal language. Even turns of phrase common in pagan Greek epitaphs occur here, such as this inscription carved on the wall of the corridor of the eastern entrance to the catacomb.

> Be of good courage, pious parents!
> No one is immortal.

An interesting example of Hellenized Judaism comes to expression in an inscription carved above the same corridor:

> Good luck for the resurrection
> of your souls.

The other Greek inscriptions in Catacomb 20 are names: Agrippa, Alypis, and Domnika "the Little." One Greek inscription is the word *Meōniton,* which evidently is an *ethnicon,* or a name indicating a place of origin. In this case the deceased is from Ma'on in Judaea. His name in Greek suggests that it is the principal language of the village.

We have already introduced the letters of Bar Kokhba in the discussion of Hebrew and Aramaic. It is therefore appropriate to cite the Greek letters here.[57] One letter to En-gedi asked for ritual paraphernalia to celebrate Succoth or Tabernacles, but designated that festival with a rather awkward phrase. The author also explained why the letter was in Greek:

So[uma]ios to Jonathan [son of] Baianos and Masabbala, Greetings. Since I have sent to you Agrippa, hurry to send me branches and citrons, and furnish them for the Citron-celebration of the Jews. And do not do otherwise. Now this has been written in Greek because a desire has not been found to write in Hebrew. Send him quickly for the feast, and do not do otherwise.

> Soumaios,
> Farewell.

His explanation that the letter was written in Greek "because a desire has not been found to write in Hebrew" suggests that Greek is Soumaios's first language and Hebrew his second or third—likely third after Aramaic—or that Greek was his only language. If the second possibility is correct, he would have used a scribe for the Hebrew form of this letter.

Who is the sender? There is some disagreement here. Some think the name is the Greek form of Simon Bar Kokhba (Bar Khosiba in the other Greek letter) and that therefore the ancient president of Israel himself wrote it. Others take it to be a non-Jewish name, as witness the phrase "of the Jews." No Jew, it seems, would feel it necessary to point out to Jews that the "Citron-celebration" is "of the Jews."

Whatever the case, Greek is surely the author's first language. It is not an elegant, educated Greek, and the handwriting is not that of a scribe. It cannot be lost on us, however, that Jonathan and Masabbala were able to read it.

The reader will recall that the same cave contained the archive of Babata, in which were twenty-four documents in

87

Greek, among others. These proved to be the legal file of this lady. It is possible to trace the vicissitudes of her life from them. Between 110 and 132 C.E., she lost her first husband, remarried a man with a grown daughter, and left a son with a guardian when she left Nabataea. The guardian proved untrustworthy. She had to go to court to guarantee proper use of two drachmas a month in support of the child. There is more, but the conclusion seems obvious. Greek was the normal language of courts and other major legal transactions. Six documents were in the Nabataean language, but only because of her Nabataean background. Fragments of Latin papyri were found in these caves, but not enough to paint a clear picture of their contents.

Latin

Latin never gained a strong foothold in Palestine outside the sphere of influence of the Roman legions and procurators. This is no surprise, since we have pointed out above that Greek was already the language of the Roman presence in the eastern empire.

The earliest evidences for Latin, however, are of the first century C.E., or almost a century after the Roman conquest in 63 B.C.E. First we have an inscription from Caesarea, now badly defaced, that mentions Pontius Pilate.[58]

....	the Tiberium
....	Pontius Pilatus
....	[Pref]ect of Judaea

It appears that the inscription dedicated a temple or other public buildings to Tiberius donated by Pontius Pilate. It may therefore be an example of the Roman ruler cult that Pilate honored here. There is thus a rationale for using Latin, especially by Pilate, who had no reputation as a Hellenophile.

This inscription must date to before 36 C.E., the year of Pilate's recall to Rome.

Another first-century Latin inscription emerged in the excavations south of the Temple in Jerusalem.[59] The text mentions the emperor Vespasian and Titus, his successor. Someone in antiquity deliberately chiseled off the name of L. Flavius Silva from the fifth line. He served as commander of the Roman Tenth Legion (the Fretensis) during its stay in Jerusalem after the devastation of the First Revolt. He also accepted the appointment of governor of the Roman province of Judaea from 73 to 79 C.E.

> EMP[eror] CAESAR
> VESPASIAN
> AUG[ustus] EMP[eror] T[itus] CAE-
> SAR VESP[asian] AUG[ustus]
> L. [FLAVIUS SILVA]
> AUG[ustus] PR[o] PR[aetor]
> LEG[ion] X [10th] FR[etensis]

Over the years many roof tiles stamped with Latin abbreviations for the Tenth Legion have come to light in Jerusalem. They usually bear variants on "LEG. X. FR." as in the last line of the column inscription above. Others have appeared near Megiddo at ancient Legio (meaning "legion").[60]

Caesarea furnishes us with another Latin inscription to be associated with a certain Cleopatra and dated after the First Revolt.[61] Vespasian granted Caesarea the rank of a Roman colony, and its title is reflected in the inscription. The same rank is recognized in another first-century inscription erected by Marcus Flavius Agrippa at Caesarea, perhaps actually a son of Josephus.[62] The title of the city is "Colonia Prima Flavia Augusta Caesarea."

Other Latin inscriptions are known from Caesarea and elsewhere, such as those that adorn the high-level aqueduct, Latin epitaphs of soldiers, and a votive altar of the Twelfth

Legion.[63] Otherwise, the inscriptions of Caesarea are overwhelmingly in Greek.

Thus Latin was clearly the specialty language of an occupying power. It appeared on milestones, because they also marked official Roman policy. Soldiers from western provinces stationed in Palestine or Judaea could not use Greek and would have had to rely on bilingual colleagues. For them Latin or their own western dialect would be the daily language. Their officers and other officials could read the Latin inscriptions.

Conclusions

It seems, then, that we can begin to chart the historical developments in the complex set of factors that describe the linguistic situation of first-century C.E. Palestine. The elements that control the patterns are not all clear, but we recognize some of them. For example, we can say that the amount of Greek known by the members of a family probably reflected their status and role in society. That is, the cultured elite would doubtless know far more Greek than the place-bound laborer. Another variable is urbanization. Much as Greek was the language of ancient Antioch but Syriac that of the surrounding farmers, so Greek was first an urban language in Judaea. It then gradually penetrated the Aramaic-speaking countryside. Yet there were probably small pockets of people everywhere who never learned Greek.

Likewise, Aramaic, at first the language of all the people, gradually suffered a decline that probably accelerated with each war against Rome. It appears that sometime during the first century B.C.E. Aramaic and Greek changed places as Greek spread into the countryside and as knowledge of Aramaic declined among the educated and among urban dwellers.

Hebrew remained alive all along, as ossuary inscriptions testify, but as a decidedly minority language. Likely also many continued to use Hebrew for reasons of Jewish pride, identity, and tradition. But Hebrew seems to have suffered a serious blow with the drop in national pride as a result of the disastrous defeat at the hands of Rome in 70 C E, followed in the next century by a brief peak and another drop as events led to the Second Revolt and its sad aftermath. Already at Beth She' arim in the second century C.E. it seemed that Hebrew had become the language of sages and scholars, while Greek continued its ascendancy as the language of prestige and status. Aramaic never died, though it suffered a strong eclipse in favor of Greek.

In view of the above-noted regionalism in Galilee, a few words must be added regarding the situation in Upper Galilee from the mid-second century to the fifth century C.E., or the heyday of the rabbinic period in Palestine. It is quite possible to interpret the paucity of Greek inscriptional data in Upper Galilee as reflecting a genuine linguistic conservatism, if not a conscious attempt to preserve a dominant Semitic cultural ambience.[4] If this be the case, the hills of Upper Galilee constitute a sort of barrier against the encroachments of Greek language and culture which prospered so greatly in other regions.

5

Jewish Burial Practices and Views of Afterlife, and Early Christian Evidences

Some of the most important archaeological material, because it may provide new insights into the world of the sages and contribute to a new perspective on that world, has to do with the field of Jewish tombs and burial customs. If we lack datable material from the Herodian period in Galilee, surely in Judaea and other parts of ancient Palestine we have a great abundance of Jewish funerary remains from this time. Given the chronological importance of such data, it is imperative to evaluate this material properly, relating it to both the growing repertoire of material culture available from this period and to the literature used to reconstruct it.

Goodenough began his monumental study of Jewish symbols with tombs, but he concentrated largely on the symbols and decoration on Jewish sarcophagi and ossuaries.[1] In keeping with the methodological assumptions noted in chapter 1, we maintain that focusing upon decoration alone is not enough. On the contrary, it is the cumulative data from all archaeological fields that will enable us to come closer to the reality of the world of the sages and of early Christianity. Art and architecture, while important, do not provide us with a perspective broad enough for evaluating either the chronological considerations which must come into play or the assumptions which governed their borrowing and adoption within the Palestinian sphere.

A parade example will help us better understand this problem. Beth She' arim is perhaps the best known and most important of ancient Palestinian cemeteries for most of the Roman period from c. 100 B.C.E. to 351 C.E.[2] It has produced some of the finest oriental art in Roman Palestine and has provided a corpus of Jewish epigraphy unsurpassed at any other single site. Were we to examine the art and architecture of Beth She' arim alone, and take note of the fact that nearly 80 percent of all the inscriptions there are Greek, we might conclude that the sages were substantially assimilated into the dominant Hellenistic culture of the day to the extent that it obliterated all traces of Semitic thought and artistic expression. However, examination in detail of both the art and the content of the inscriptions, as well as study of the burial customs employed there, suggests a far richer alternative explanation.

To be sure, the rabbis and their families were at home with Greek, but not to the extent that they surrendered the biblical or Semitic view of afterlife.[3] In addition, figural representations of mythic scenes on sarcophagi suggest an acquaintance with dominant Roman artistic expression, but sufficient evidence exists for its orientalizing character.[4] The reburial of Jews from the Diaspora and elsewhere in Palestine indicates the lingering significance of the family burial ground tradition if not the importance of burial or reburial in Eretz Israel.[5]

Beth She' arim, which affords us a rich glimpse of life into Middle Roman times, impresses upon us the need to proceed in our investigations with caution and thoroughness. It also alerts us to the important consideration that while Hellenization may appear to have triumphed in the rabbinic period, such a victory may have impinged more upon the externals of Jewish life than on the inner workings of religion and culture. We will return to this theme especially in chapter 7, when we evaluate more comprehensively the evidence from art and architecture as a whole. Suffice it to say for now that the

93

dichotomous view of Goodenough that the Hellenization of Judaism in Greco-Roman Palestine, in which the external manifestations of material culture signify a new kind of Judaism removed from the leadership of the sages, is no longer adequate to explain the great array of material which has come to light in recent decades.

Jewish Tombs

It is important that we clarify at the outset the terminology we shall be using. In the present context we speak of "Jewish tombs" simply because we are unable to identify positively early Christian tombs or Jewish-Christian tombs. While some pagan tombs of the Hellenistic and Roman periods have been uncovered, the vast majority of excavated material has been from the major excavations in Jerusalem and environs that has been identified as Jewish. It is possible to speak with some surety of "Christian" tombs after Constantine, however, and in particular of Christian veneration of holy places, the most famous of which is the Grotto of the Church of the Holy Sepulchre. As for the so-called Christian ossuaries and Jewish-Christian ossuaries at Dominus Flevit on the Mount of Olives, and many other places, we will consider them below.

By the turn of the common era several major modifications in tomb construction and burial technique had come to prominence in ancient Palestine. The first and most obvious detail is the appearance of the individual receptacle for the dead, the coffin. While to the modern reader such an item may seem unimportant, for the ancient Semitic world it represented a new departure which no doubt reflected an increasing preoccupation with afterlife as well as a growing receptivity to non-Palestinian modes of inhumation. Wooden sarcophagi are well known in the Hellenistic world and, only just recently, excavations in the necropolis of ancient Jewish Jericho (Tell Abu el-Alayiq-North) produced the largest group of wooden coffins ever found in Palestine. When one considers that the individual receptacle for the dead was adopted at approximately the same time (the late Hellenistic period) as the individual loculus grave, or *kokh* (a burial shaft cut horizontally back into the wall of a tomb chamber), one has the distinct impression that such diversity in tomb architecture and manner of disposition of the dead reflects the growing variety in the religous views of the same era.[6] Any number of variations are associated with the adoption of the loculus grave. Especially dominant, however, is the arcosolium tomb, in which the roof of the shelf is cut in the shape of an arch. Still another variant form is the pit grave, a simple niche or loculus that is cut into the floor of a tomb.

There has been much speculation surrounding the burial practices in Jewish tombs because of the fact that evidence of both primary burial (one in which the corpse remains in its original position) and secondary burial (one in which skeletal remains are reburied in some manner) has been found in such diverse contexts. Unfortunately, some earlier excavations paid little attention to skeletal remains, and it is often difficult to assess the nature of those burials. Nonetheless, several generalizations may be made. Ossuaries, or short coffins (around eighty centimeters) are universally regarded as receptacles for skeletal remains for reburial. Long coffins, or sarcophagi (around 1.8 meters), are usually for primary burials, though they are often used to receive multiple secondary burials.

In the cases where we find loculi and ossuaries, it is generally assumed that primary burial took place in the loculus and that secondary burial of the same individual was effected through the use of the ossuary, thereby freeing badly needed space and adhering to an apparently venerated custom. In tombs very often a bone chamber is found where skeletal remains are stored en masse or where ossuaries are grouped together. Since secondary burials predominate at Beth She' arim and other sites of the Late Roman and Byzantine period (e.g., Meiron and Khirbet Shema'),[7] it may now be assumed that the custom of secondary burial persisted throughout the talmudic period. While there is no mention of secondary burial in the New Testament, the fact that the Greek Orthodox church follows this practice to this day and that the cult of martyrs—reburial of the remains of holy men—gained ascendancy in the early church and in Eastern churches in particular, suggests that the custom was well known in the early Christian era. That some families practice primary burial only and others secondary burial need not disturb us unduly, since variety in such matters occurs throughout the ancient period. Analogously, while primary burial clearly is the dominant pattern of burial in America today, increasing numbers of people are employing cremation as an appropriate and acceptable means of disposition of the dead. Cremation in the Semitic or biblical world, however, was strictly forbidden, because it smacked of heathen rites and because so much status was accorded to proper burial of normal desiccated remains. With the emphasis on natural decomposition, there was consequently no place for cremation.

In noting such technical aspects of inhumation, we should like to stress that these procedures for disposing of the dead reflect a deep conservatism. Rapid burial has always been a major feature of the religions of ancient Palestine, and this custom is based on the injunction in the Pentateuch not to leave the corpse of an executed person overnight upon a tree (Deut. 21:22-23). Surely climatic factors are involved in so strong a feeling for rapid disposition of the dead, because bodies in a warm climate begin to deteriorate rapidly after expiration. Embalming too is strictly forbidden according to biblical law, and it is to this day mostly forbidden in Jewish religious practice.[8] In Egypt the cult of the dead was so developed that extensive measures beyond embalming were taken to ensure proper passage to and safekeeping in the next world. No doubt the injunction is a kind of polemic against ancient Egyptian practice, but it is also very much a positive statement in behalf of the natural process of decomposition, an adherence to the biblical adage, ashes to ashes, dust to dust (see Gen. 3:19 and Eccles. 12:7).

By New Testament times increasing importance was attached to rapid burial, to the point that leaving a corpse unburied through the night was considered disrespectful. Only in the case when extra time was required to prepare shrouds or the coffin itself, or when additional time was required for the arrival of a close relative, could actual burial be postponed. In the instance of the death of Ananias, the husband of Sapphira, burial was effected three hours after death (Acts 5:6-10). In the instance of the death of Jesus, rapid burial was even more urgent, since it occurred the day before the Sabbath a day when burial could not be carried out. (According to John 19:31 it was also the first day of Passover.) It is noteworthy too that in the case of crucifixion new evidence suggests that the victims of such torture had their legs broken, constituting a kind of merciful act or *coup de grâce* to abbreviate their suffering.[9] Recent remains of a crucified male from Jerusalem indicate that he was reburied in an ossuary after first being interred in a family tomb. The noncanonical rabbinic tractate *Semahot* records that special provisions were made for families of individuals executed in such a manner (*Semahot* 2.11), while the Mishnah records that a special gravesite was set aside for executed criminals (*Sanhedrin* 6.5).

According to Jewish law, preparation for primary burial included washing the body, annointing it with oil (presumably to perfume the body), and wrapping it in shrouds. The order of annointing/washing is ambiguous in the Jewish sources,[10] and the Gospel accounts apparently reflect this confusion (cf. Mark 16:1; Luke 7:38; John 12:3, with John 11:2 and Acts 9:37). Jesus' body was "bound in linen clothes with spices, as was the burial custom of the Jews." Spices could well have been used to provide a pleasant odor in the hot Mediterranean climate, thereby rendering death more acceptable, but the reference could also be to the simple custom of sprinkling spices on the funeral bier or to the practice of burning them along the route of the funeral procession (see Mark 16:1; Luke

24:1). Jewish tradition is explicit in indicating that men may wrap and bind men in these shrouds but the women could bind both men and women (*Semahot* 12.10).

The return of the women to Jesus' grave the following morning may indicate that there had not been sufficient time to wash and annoint his body properly the day before the Sabbath (Luke 23:55-56; 24:1-3), and Jewish law further provides that the preparation of the body itself is permissible even on the Sabbath (*m. Shabbat* 23.5). Another interpretation of the return of the women to the grave and the rolling away of the stone is that they came to ascertain whether he was really dead, a genuine fear which is attested by several sources. While we have noted how much more frequently the coffin came to be used in this period, in the rock-cut tombs with loculi and arcosolia that we find in the Jerusalem area, primary burial could well have been simply in a knit covering inserted directly into the carved receptacle in the soft limestone.[11] Jewish literature suggests that in many instances no coffin was used at all, "out of respect to the poor" (*b. Moed Qatan* 27*b*). Burial in a Jerusalem tomb would not have involved any shoveling of dirt but would have meant the insertion of the wrapped corpse into a burial slot that might or might not be sealed. The entire tomb complex was closed or sealed with a rolling stone or hinged stone door.

Semitic preoccupation with proper burial dates back to earliest biblical days, when the patriarchs were concerned that their remains be interred in Canaan and in the family tomb.[11a] As in the later periods, the early biblical era attests both to primary and to secondary inhumation as regular forms of disposing of the dead. And it is the tradition of being "gathered to one's people" or "sleeping with one's fathers" that governed the idea that a family or extended family be buried together. Reunion in death somehow took away something of death's sting, and burial in a rock-cut subterranean chamber reflects the earlier biblical view of death as it relates to Sheol.[11b] Thus there is enormous continuity in the postbiblical manner of disposing of the dead attested by both Jewish and Christian sources.

It is quite clear, however, that reburial in the Greco-Roman period is associated with the most developed Semitic view of afterlife, namely, resurrection, as well as with a more diffuse merger between Semitic and Greek views of afterlife. Resurrection too need not be understood in its most narrowly defined terms but rather as a category of thought which presupposed a postmortem existence not entirely unrelated to life. In Semitic thought the bodily process of decomposition was viewed as both a positive and a natural stage in human development which should be treated as reverentially as birth. Despite extensive rulings of law to guard against defilement of the dead, secondary burial became more and more common and in its final stages provides vivid testimony to Jewish attachment to burial on holy soil and to the expiatory effects of decomposition itself. Without epigraphic evidence, however, it is difficult to indicate what a particular burial or group of burials means. That is why Beth She'arim has become so important in understanding the development of views of afterlife in the Roman period.

Suffice it to say that the quintessential Semitic thought pattern saw man as a total entity, a solitary unit. Man's soul was regarded not as an intangible entity but rather as the constitutive essence of an individual. There is no dualistic view of man in Hebrew Scripture, and such a conception of man entered into Jewish considerations of afterlife only after the rise of Hellenism and the experience of and exposure to a century or so of late Greek thinking. It was only after this blending of cultures that the rabbis showed any receptivity to modifying their dominant view of resurrection in the light of Hellenistic views. By tannaitic times, or the first centuries of the common era, at least some of the rabbis departed from the previous notion of the soul as "total individual" in favor of a view of the soul as an independent entity that transcends death.

Nonetheless, despite the penetration of the Greek view of immortality of the soul, the rabbis never quite succeeded in creating a coherent system of thought which blended the Greek with the Semitic. What resulted was the juxtaposition of disparate views. That is why rabbinic views of death cannot be simplified or harmonized into a single, definite system of thought. While it is difficult to pinpoint when in the late Hellenistic or Roman period this admixture of theological systems began, it is possible to place it between the period of the flourishing of the Jewish community of Alexandria in the first century B.C.E. and the period after the Second Roman War in the second century C.E. It is clear, however, that the New Testament emphasis on resurrection of the dead, as derived from the traditions in the Gospels of the empty tomb and postresurrection appearances, coincides precisely with the dominant view of main-line Jewish thought which incorporated the benedictions for revivification of the dead into the heart of their liturgy very close to the time of the transmission of the New Testament itself.[11c]

Beth She' arim

The excavations at Beth She' arim have vastly increased our knowledge of Jewish architecture and art in the period of the Mishnah and the Talmud, known heretofore mainly from the synagogues in Palestine and neighboring countries, and from the catacombs in Rome. Much new knowledge of burial practices was obtained, as well as of Judeo-Greek, Hebrew, and Aramaic epigraphy. The new finds in all these fields are a considerable contribution to Talmudic research and to that of the social, religious, and economic aspects of the period of the Mishnah and the Talmud.[12]

In chapter 4 we adduced the relative significance of Beth She' arim for understanding the languages of ancient Palestine. It should be clear from the above statement that

Beth She' arim also provides a vivid glimpse into the burial customs of the sages and greatly illuminates our understanding of views of afterlife in Roman Palestine. It is incredible to think that this necropolis, which has provided such riches of literary material to the student of ancient Palestine, has yet to be fully appreciated or even studied outside the modern state of Israel. It is hoped that the following brief statement, the remarks in chapter 4, and the remarks in chapter 7 pertaining to the art of late antiquity will contribute to a better appreciation of one of the premier sites of ancient Palestine.

Known in the literature also by its Arabic name, Sheikh Ibreik, the Beth She' arim report is now fully available to English readers in a lavish three-volume publication of the Israel Exploration Society. The fact that it was available hitherto in Hebrew only (except for very specialized and individualized studies) has led to its limited readership. Clearly this is what hampered Goodenough's valuable but limited assessment of the material in his pioneering work on the material culture of Jewish antiquity. Both Goodenough and other scholars failed to understand Beth She' arim as a burial center for Jews of the Diaspora as well as for Jews of Palestine; few have appreciated the import of the fact that secondary burials predominate at Beth She' arim and hence provide witness to the customs and beliefs of Jews from all over the Eastern Mediterranean world.

Since the variety of types of burial at Beth She' arim is consistent with what we have found in Jerusalem, it will not be necessary to describe them here. We should underscore, however, that many elaborate rooms were used simply to store collected bone remains (e.g., Room II of Catacomb 1), while other rooms served as stores for ossuaries and coffins, the latter often functioning as large ossuaries for multiple secondary burials.

While nearly 80 percent of the epigraphs at Beth She' arim are in Greek, we have already indicated that it is not always a simple task to assess the true importance of a funerary inscription. To be sure, adoption of the Greek language contributed to a subtle shift in the psychological perceptions of those who commissioned, spoke, or dictated the epigraphs. Yet it is another matter to evaluate how these brief statements reflect upon the dynamic thought system of the Jewish world at that time. A recent study has attempted to deal with this question in a forthright and compelling way. In distinguishing between formulas which are merely Greek versions of Jewish ideas and those which were pagan in origin but later came into Jewish usage, Senzo Nagakubo has concluded the following:

> As regards the formulas of the first group, attempts to find in them particular Greek notions of afterlife have proven quite futile. We must rest content in saying that as a whole the substance as well as sentiment embodied in them is basically Semitic, and to be more specific, Jewish when the belief in resurrection is explicitly or implicitly stated. The formulas of the second group, on the other hand, have provided a basis from which to build a strong case for Jewish assimilation of the Hellenistic notions of afterlife. These formulas were no mere Greek versions of Hebrew ideas; they were consciously borrowed from their pagan neighbors. Undoubtedly, the precise implications which these formulas conjured up in the minds of the Jews were not quite identical with those which were present in the minds of the pagans because the religious system of each was different. Moreover, it is quite likely that the Jews consciously modified pagan elements they found to be incompatible with their religous beliefs. For instance, no matter how rampant the notion of the deification in the heavenly realm of the souls of the departed was among the pagans, it was never acceptable to the Jewish mentality because of their understanding of man as a creature of God.[13]

On the basis of a complete study of all the Greek inscriptions at Beth She' arim, Nagakubo further concludes that it is impossible to say that the Jews of the Diaspora were any more or less Hellenized than those from Eretz Israel. In fact, in Catacomb 20, where the rabbinic leadership of Beth She' arim was interred, both the notion of resurrection of the dead and immortality of the soul are poignantly juxtaposed. This datum will help us greatly when we come to assess more of the evidence from art, so often understood as reflecting a separate Hellenized element within Jewish life.

Early Christian Evidences

If at Beth She' arim we have an abundance of material with which to work, the opposite is true with respect to material from early Christianity until the establishment of Christianity by Constantine the Great. Part of the reason for this state of affairs is the tacit assumption in New Testament circles that the Jewish-Christian church fled to Transjordan during the First Revolt and particularly to Pella of the Decapolis. While the Italian Franciscans have labored to identify the material culture of that Palestinian Jewish-Christian movement, it is not yet possible to accept either their methodological assumptions or their data. On the other hand, sufficient data do exist to warrant a more serious exploration of such a possibility, especially in view of recent discoveries of Capernaum.[14] The presence of so many churches so soon after Constantine suggests a base other than rabbinic Judaism from which the early church was built.

About thirty years ago a sensation was created in the archaeological world when ossuaries discovered in Jerusalem were announced to be the earliest traces of Christianity because cross marks had been found on them. Because the names inscribed on these bone repositories reflected the names of the New Testament, many were inclined to accept the Christian designation without much critical scrutiny.[15] A similar claim had been made in the late nineteenth century with respect to names of a later date. While a great deal of criticism has since emerged, the Italian Franciscan scholars

Bagatti, Testa, and Mancini, and the French Jesuit Danielou have carried on the argument for the Jewish-Christian identification of some cross marks. Others have argued that they are *tav* marks, functioning as a Jewish religious symbol in the early centuries.[16]

Without rehearsing many of the extensive arguments on this subject, we state our concurrence with those scholars who regard the marks as artisan signs intended to indicate matching places between lid and receptacle, and conveying the simple meaning "this is the spot."[17] Because ossuaries often were crudely made, it is helpful to have such spots indicated to facilitate the closing of the lid after the bones had been deposited. It is our opinion that ossuaries in general cannot be understood solely by their ornament or decoration. Rather, it is the burial custom which underlies the phenomenon and the epigraphy sometimes on the ossuaries that provide the most promising avenues for understanding the people who were buried in them. It is interesting to note, however, that art historians who have examined the ornament of ossuaries have indicated an Eastern influence to the decoration, something which well accords with the borrowed eastern Semitic vocabulary (e.g., *kokh*) for secondary burial.[18]

Robert Houston Smith, the excavator of Pella, has recently advanced another line of argument with regard to Jewish-Christian evidence based on his own work in the Byzantine church at Pella.[19] We include discussion of his work here because it centers on his analysis of a large sarcophagus uncovered in the north apse of the West Church in a burial crypt, or cist. On the basis of comparisons with similar sarcophagi found in datable contexts, Smith concludes that the Pella sarcophagus was executed between 60 and 135 C.E., precisely the time when Jewish Christians flourished there. He further maintains that were it a reliquary of the Byzantine era, that is, a coffin in which venerated remains were preserved, it would have been visible within the church. Moreover, since this kind of sarcophagus is usually found with ossuaries, it has a Jewish connection.

Smith comes to the conclusion that the West Church could hardly have been erected without knowledge of the presence of the cist, which was probably part of a larger cemetery or possibly a mausoleum. Therefore, the church was positioned in such a way as to include the cist, which he further concludes must have functioned as a kind of repository of saint's remains, in this instance, deriving directly from the early Jewish-Christian community of Pella, possibly of an individual who had contact with Jesus' disciples or with Jesus himself. It should be readily discernible that such a line of inquiry is very strained and that the evidence for Smith's conclusions is indirect at best. It is our opinion that the case of Pella and the early Jewish-Christian community there has yet to be made. One hopes that Smith's and Hennessey's new excavations in Pella will help to clarify the archaeological aspect of the Jewish-Christian presence.

Were we to enter into a discussion of the building stages of the Church of the Holy Sepulchre, we would begin in the year of 326 C E. when Constantine planned the first basilica and conclude with the restoration efforts of the Greek, Latin, and Armenian church authorities, which began in 1959 and continue to the present. In any case, the church today is being restored. The original intent was to return it to the state it was in when the Latins rededicated it in 1149. All who have visited the church can clearly understand how the edifice is meant to commemorate the tomb of Jesus, and presumably the site of his crucifixion, Golgotha, as well.[20] There is another Jewish tomb eighteen meters from the Sepulchre. It is of the *kokh* type discussed above. This simply underscores the significance of building the first church on one specific tomb among several and places the erection of the Constantinian church squarely in the tradition of the veneration of holy places and events, which more properly belongs to our discussion of churches in chapter 6.

In regard to the Church of the Holy Sepulchre, however, a recent excavation by Magen Broshi in the eastern extremity of the Armenian Quarter known as Saint Helena's Chapel has brought forward the earliest pre-Constantinian evidence of pilgrimage to one of the venerated tombs thought to be the tomb of Jesus. The most startling find of this small excavation was a "boldly drawn red and black graffiti [sic] of a small Roman sailing vessel."[21] Beneath the drawing is the inscription *"DOMINE IVIMUS"* ("Lord, we went"), possibly a reference to the pilgrim Psalm 122, which begins: "Let us go to the house of the Lord." The excavator dates the inscription to the year 330 C.E. during which time construction was being conducted on the Constantinian church. While we know of earlier Christian pilgrimages, it is significant to note this artifact in connection with the putative tomb of Jesus and the Church of the Holy Sepulchre.

With Constantine's conversion in 324 C.E. the cross as a Christian symbol may be taken for granted.[22] If this symbol facilitates our ability to identify Christian artifacts, it nonetheless forces us again to consider the possibility of the persistence of Jewish Christianity in Palestine. Indeed, in a published tomb from Gush Halav, Gischala of Josephus in the Galilee, at least some American scholars are now willing to believe that the cross symbol uncovered there may well provide evidence of Jewish-Christians, or the *minim* of the Talmud.[23] The context of this tomb is clearly late fourth century and hence raises many substantive questions regarding the persistence of a local form of Palestinian Christianity as well as the general question of relations between the early church and rabbinic Judaism.

Our search for early Christian evidences must also lead us to Nazareth, which was most recently excavated from 1955 to 1960 by the Franciscans.[24] Here Bagatti, the excavator, found a series of Christian churches and other remains beneath the Basilica of the Annunciation. These include, in reverse chronological order, a crusader church, a fourth or fifth-century Byzantine church, and an earlier edifice, probably prior to the fourth century. This building was of plain white and painted plaster and featured columns about fifty-five centimeters in diameter, with their bases resting upon a stylobate. The architectural fragments resemble those from synagogues stratigraphically excavated at Khirbet Shema', Meiron, and Gush Halav in Upper Galilee.[25] These are known to have been founded about the middle of the third century C.E., which is the date assigned by the excavators to the Nazareth building.[26] The pre-Byzantine building also contained many graffiti in Greek, though also in Syriac, Aramaic, and one in Armenian. The building is oriented north to south. More could be said, but the main point is that the graffiti appear to be Christian in character. Thus the excavators feel that this is likely a Jewish-Christian synagogue. The multilingual graffiti represent the scratchings of Christian pilgrims who have come to venerate a place sacred to Christian memory.[27]

Exactly under the nave of the Byzantine church was a basin with seven steps that is most reasonably interpreted as a ritual bath, or *mikveh*.[28] It is not oriented with the walls of the Byzantine church or with the walls of the earlier putative Jewish-Christian synagogue, which implies that it predates both structures. As it now stands, it is impossible to date. Yet it is provocative to think that this may be one of the earliest pieces of Jewish-Christian architecture.

Despite the fact that there is little or no consensus among scholars today regarding the manner of identifying such remains as Jewish or Jewish-Christian, the authors are hopeful that the present work will enable a new set of criteria accessible to all to evolve. We hope the availability of such criteria will propel the field of early Christian archaeology into an era in which new historical breakthroughs may be achieved.[29]

Conclusions

A cursory review of some of the data that has emanated from Jewish tombs of Roman Palestine indicates once again the promise of the archaeological-literary approach. A study of both the literary traditions and of the material remains suggests the extent of the imprint of these burial customs on the total culture. In fact, there is every evidence of a close continuum between the Jews of Palestine and the Jews of the Diaspora. A study of those funerary inscriptions from Beth She' arim that are in Greek has shown that Semitic and Hellenistic views of afterlife are so closely interwoven that the mere dominance of the Greek language is not sufficient to indicate the degree of accommodation to Hellenism.

Close attention to the details of burial further enables one to evaluate more carefully the meaning and context of ancient tombs and will eventually illuminate even further aspects of the socioeconomic situation. The lack of scholarly consensus and the inadequacies of method among those who study Jewish Christianity prevent us from concluding anything of substance on this elusive matter. Jewish Christianity remains one of the most tantalizing of all questions in the study of Christian origins, and because so much of the data purported to be Jewish-Christian is artifactual in nature, we sincerely hope that greater attention will be paid to pertinent discussion of it in the future.

The question of early Christian evidences is intimately tied to the study of Jewish tombs. Insofar as some of the earliest veneration of Christian holy places involved grottoes and tombs, it is imperative for the student of this subject to be knowledgeable in Jewish funerary customs. The Jewish custom of secondary reburial in Eretz Israel may well constitute a kind of paradigm for early Christian pilgrims, for it is in the church that the cult of martyrs and reliquaries took strongest root. That rabbinic patterns of inhumation influenced Christian burial customs, and even the religious framework for the reestablishment of the church in Palestine, shows how deeply interdependent church and synagogue were in their most formative period. That such a situation might obtain in a period of supposed animosity between Jew and Christian indicates the extent to which these communities remained in close contact.

Fig. 1. Localities mentioned in *Archaeology, the Rabbis, and Early Christianity.*

If a town has an O.T. and N.T. name, both are included.
• City, Village, etc.
+ O.T. city only
[HAIFA] modern name only. Some sites are in modern Arabic only.

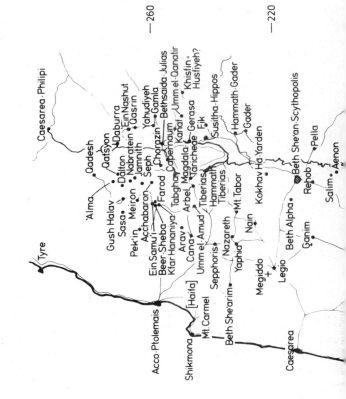

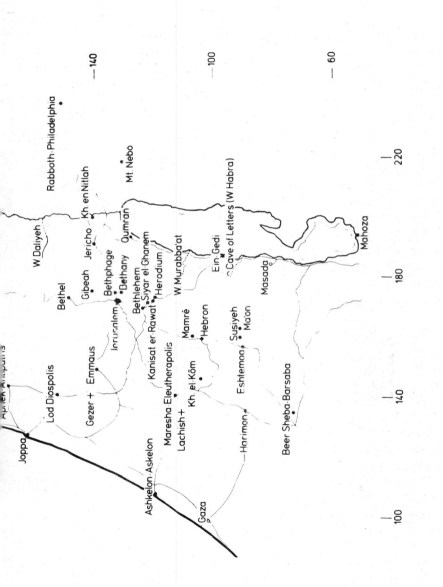

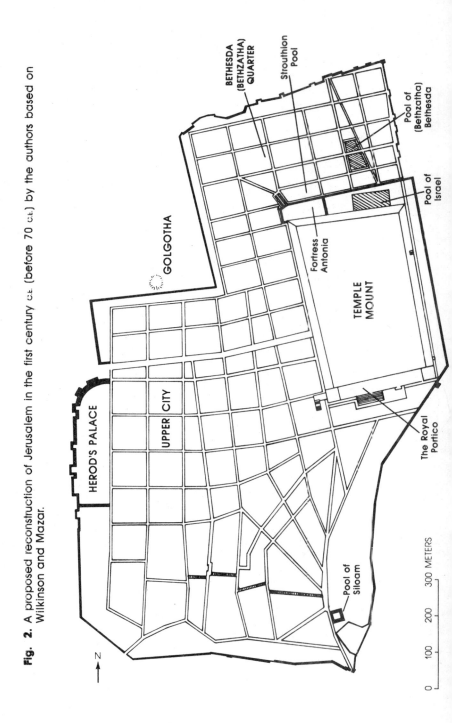

Fig. 2. A proposed reconstruction of Jerusalem in the first century c.e. (before 70 c.e.) by the authors based on Wilkinson and Mazar.

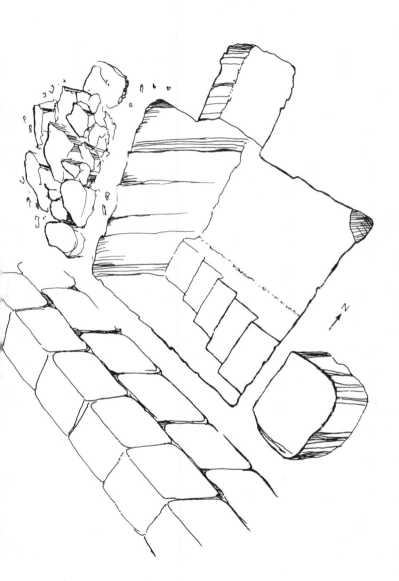

Fig. 3. Nazareth: Ritual bath, or *mikveh*, from beneath the Church of the Annunciation. To the left is the wall of the presumed Jewish-Christian synagogue revised as the south stylobate of the fifth-century C.E. church.

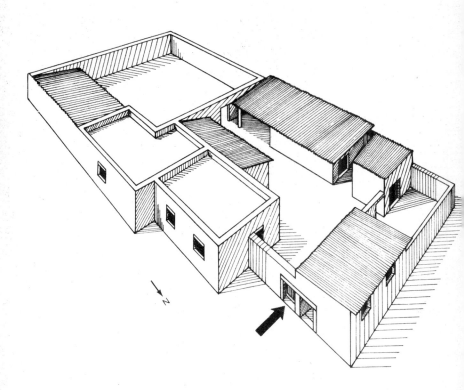

Fig. 4. "St. Peter's House" at Capernaum. Perspective reconstruction
from the northeast. Arrow points to the entrance
to the courtyard.

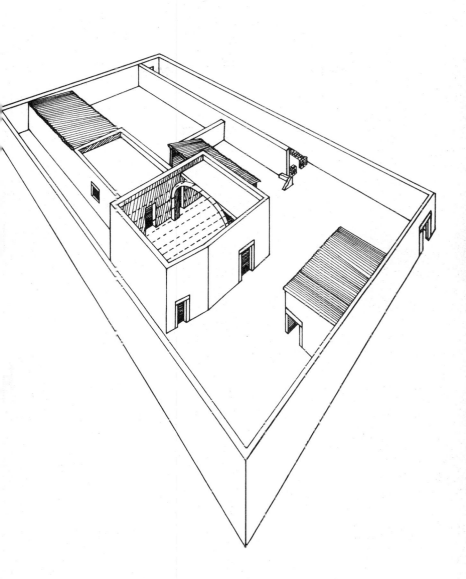

Fig. 5. Perspective reconstruction from the same angle of the house-church at Capernaum, built directly on the main room of "St. Peter's House."

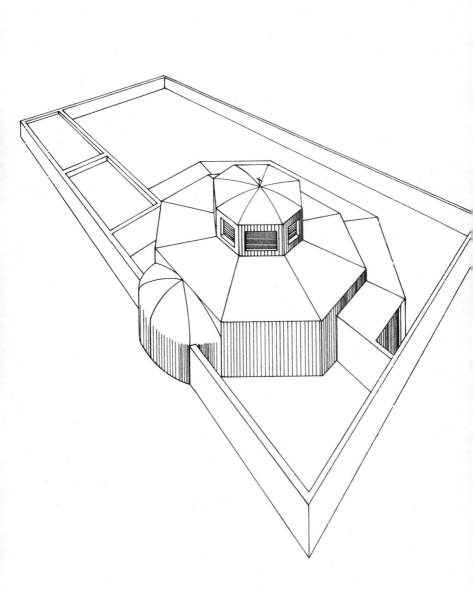

Fig. 6. Perspective reconstruction from the same angle of the fifth-century octagonal church built over the remains of the house-church.

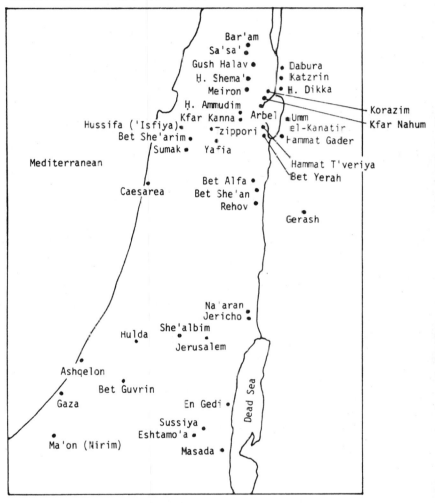

Fig. 7. Location map of major synagogues in Eretz Israel.

Fig. 8. Selection of synagogue ground plans adapted from Avi-Yonah.

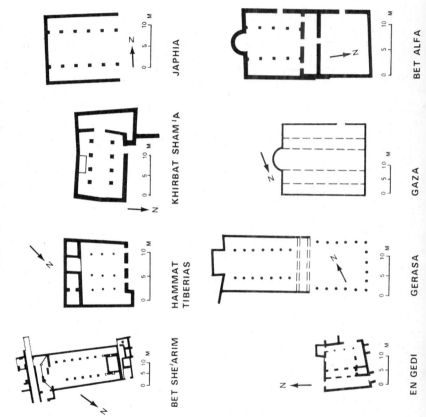

BET SHE'ARIM

HAMMAT TIBERIAS

KHIRBAT SHAM'A

JAPHIA

EN GEDI

GERASA

GAZA

BET ALFA

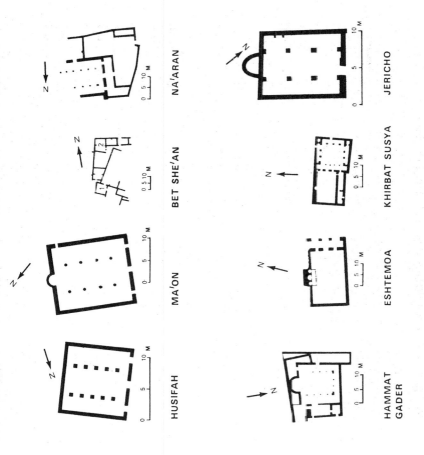

HUSIFAH

MA'ON

BET SHE'AN

NA'ARAN

HAMMAT
GADER

ESHTEMOA

KHIRBAT SUSYA

JERICHO

Fig. 9. Perspective and cutaway of synagogue at Khirbet Shema'.

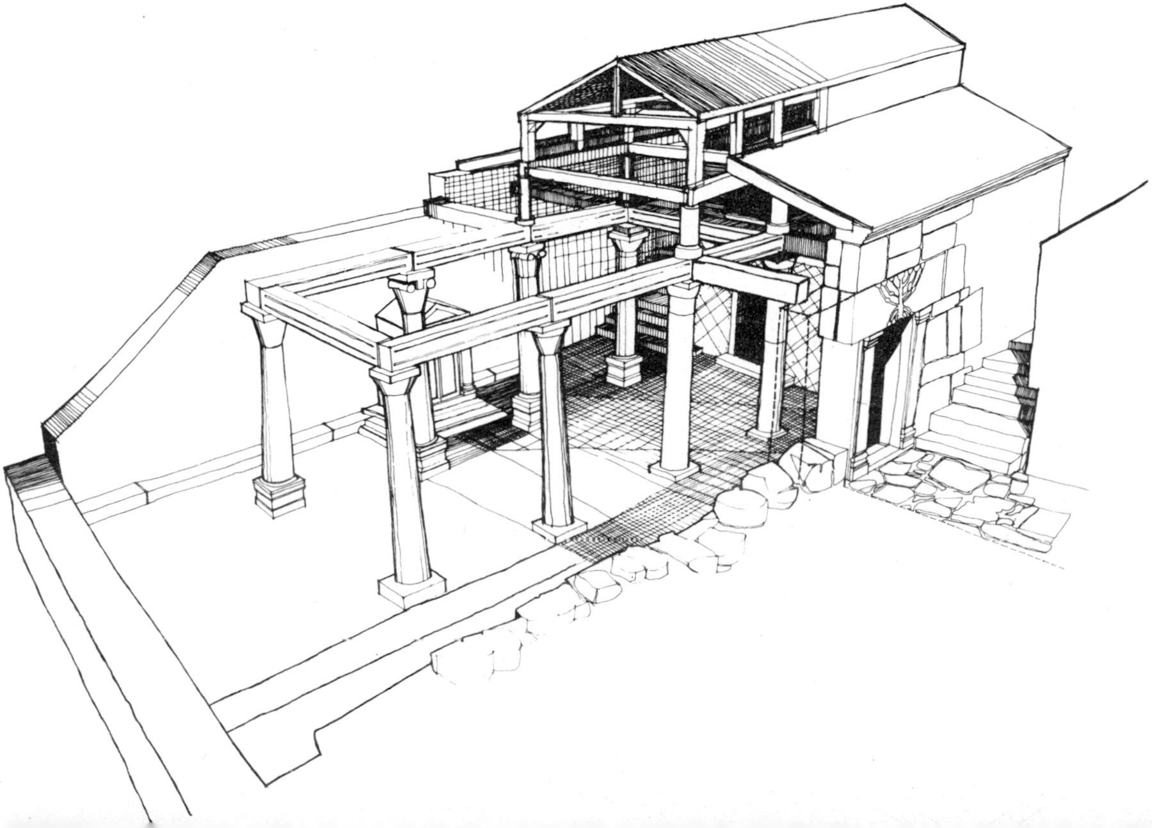

Fig. 10. Reconstruction drawing of synagogue at Khirbet Shema' with House of Study at right.

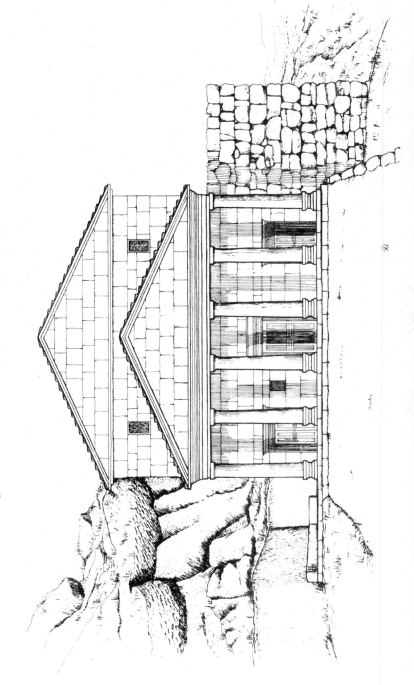

Fig. 11. Reconstructed facade of ancient synagogue at Meiron.

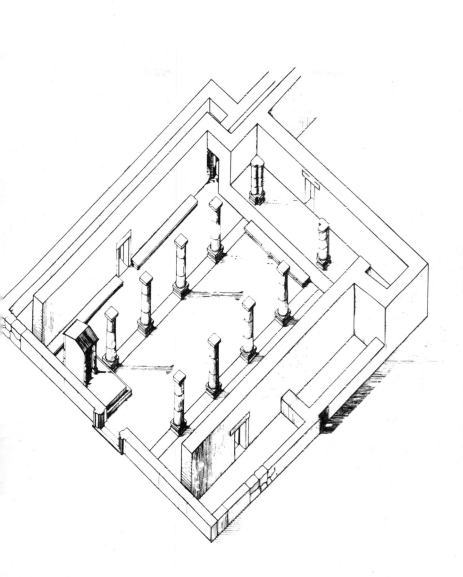

Fig. 12. Gush Halav synagogue.

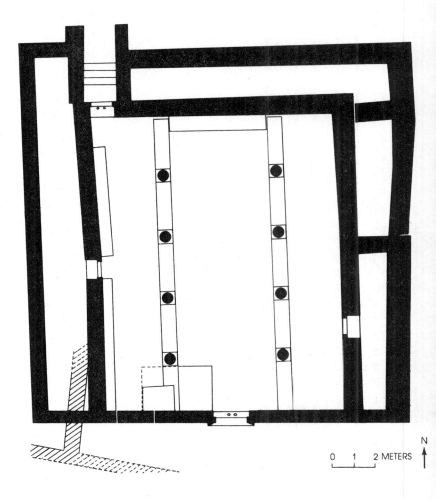

0   1   2 METERS

N

Fig. 13. Block plan of Gush Halav synagogue.

6

Evidences of Early Christianity:
Churches in the
Holy Land

It has long been a truism in the study of early Christianity
that if we were to depend solely on archaeological evidence we
might conclude that Christianity sprang full-grown from the
head of Constantine in the fourth century C.E. This is so
because the amount of evidence that is surely Christian from
the early centuries is small indeed. It is also true that no one is
certain how to interpret the archaeological data that has been
recovered, so that assigning it to early Christianity is quite
problematic. In other words, the problem of methodology is
particularly acute here, as is the question of proper
interpretation.

As we have said before, the Christian movement did not
develop a fixed repertoire of symbols, iconography, architecture, and cultic paraphernalia until well past the first century,
some would even say as late as the fourth century.[1] In our
effort to isolate early Christian evidences, therefore, we move
into a dim no-man's-land. Our task may be ameliorated
somewhat if we take it as an operating hypothesis that the
movement in its earliest stages was too heterogeneous for us
to recognize any single monument or artifact as uniquely
Christian. In other words, taking our clue from the social
historians of early Christianity,[2] the very diversity of ethnic

elements, language groups, social classes, etc. represented in the new "Jesus movement"[3] militates against our identifying with certainty those elements of the material culture that are "Christian."

What, then, are we to do? Perhaps the simplest method is to move backward from certainty to less certainty, from the known to the unknown. In other words, perhaps we can look at the phenomenon of Christian churches in the Holy Land in the fourth century and work backward, even if only a bit, into that no-man's-land that has yet to be defined.

The Evidence

With this note of caution, we find that we can provisionally identify almost thirty places in the Holy Land with Christian remains of the fourth century C.E., or localities where we expect to find them because of literary notices.[4] These include the Constantinian edifices at Bethlehem (the Church of the Nativity) and Jerusalem (the churches of the Holy Sepulchre, the Mount of Olives—Eleona—and the Ascension). These two localities were of special interest to Helena, mother of Constantine.

At least one other site reflects Constantine's intervention. Evidently a pre-Christian, not necessarily Jewish, sanctuary existed at Mamre—sacred for its association with the appearance of the angel of the Lord to Abraham (Gen. 18). Eutropia, Constantine's mother-in-law, was offended by the pagan nature of the worship there and asked Constantine to intervene. He pulled down the statues and the altar and built a church.[5] This basilica occupied the eastern side of an enclosure that dates as early as Herod or Hadrian (between 37 B.C.E. and 135 C.E.).[6]

Many of these churches were associated with some event in the life of Jesus. For example, at Tabgha (Heptapegon), or Seven Springs, on the northwest shore of the Sea of Galilee stood three fourth-century churches. These memorialized the sites of the feeding of the five thousand (the Church of the Multiplication of the Loaves and Fishes),[7] of the Sermon on the Mount (the Church of the Beatitudes),[8] and the postresurrection appearance of Jesus in the Gospel of John (Mensa Christi).[9] On Mount Tabor, worshipers gathered at the church commemorating the Transfiguration.[10] In Sychar was a church at Jacob's well above the meeting place of the Samaritan woman (John 4).[11]

Christians also built churches in celebration of gospel events at places Jesus never visited: At Emmaus there may have been a house-church of Cleopas in 386, and at Siyar el-Ghanem near Bethlehem there was a monastery and church of the fourth or fifth century, evidently associated with the shepherds at Jesus' birth. One kilometer away at Kanisat er-Rawat was another cave and chapel probably associated with the same event.[12] So we know that Christians were venerating spots associated with some event in the life of Christ, their Lord. These sites appear to have been honored as *loca* of epiphanies.

We also have a notice in Epiphanius (*Adv. Haer.* 30.11) that Count Joseph of Tiberias received permission from Constantine to build churches in Tiberias, Sepphoris (Diocaesarea), Scythopolis, Nazareth, and Capernaum. Joseph complained that he had many troubles with the local populace in his attempts to convert the temple of Hadrian in Tiberias to a church, so he contented himself with a chapel. Archaeology has uncovered no traces of these structures, unless the fourth-century "house-church" at Capernaum is the result of his efforts.[13]

Other churches emphasized the continuity of local traditions by celebrating events in the Pentateuch. Egeria mentions a Church of Saint Jacob at Bethel.[14] Both Egeria and Jerome (?) report a church at Gibeah of Phinehas (Josh. 24:33).[15] The church at Khirbet en-Nitla on the Jordan is evidently Byzantine Gilgal.[16] Finally, there is the Monastery of the Bush on Mount Sinai mentioned by Egeria and the present Saint Katherine's, which contains fourth-century masonry.[17] The latter churches seem mainly to be celebrations of theophanies. Here, respectively, Jacob wrestled with the angel of the Lord; Eleazar the son of Aaron was buried; Israel crossed the Jordan; and the Lord appeared to Moses. Evidently for Christians the events of Scripture, including the New Testament, were all of a single garment.[18]

Since the building of churches was so widespread in the fourth century, and not necessarily at the hand of Constantine, we might expect to find local churches or other types of sanctuaries (house-churches or caves) prior to this pivotal century. Although remains are scanty and difficult to assess, we can make mention of a few places.

Capernaum

We have already described the house at Capernaum, which evidently was venerated by Christians before the fourth century. In this connection it may be important to summarize the excavators' conclusions about the date of the founding of the house-church and its use prior to the major rebuilding in the fourth century. But first some explanatory remarks.

The large room that lies directly under the central octagon of the fifth-century church is numbered "1" by the excavators (see figs. 4-6). The Christian community converted that room into a small church in the fourth century. Egeria saw its completed form. Thus we have three occupational periods: (1) the founding and use of the house from the first century B.C.E. to the fourth century C.E.; (2) its conversion in the fourth century into a new structure, based on the foundations of the old walls, evidently now used as a church; and (3) its destruction and the rebuilding on its remains of an octagonal church of the fifth century. In what follows, we are concerned with the detailed history of the first period.

Room 1 connects to the north with Courtyard 5-6. The question to which the excavators addressed themselves is, Did

Room 1 exist from the founding of the house, or is it the result of later rebuilding? In other words, what is the stratigraphic relation of the courtyard to Room 1 and the relative chronology of the whole? Furthermore, since Pavement B (a cobbled pavement elsewhere in this building) is to be dated to the Early Roman period, are the three plastered floors east of and above Pavement B to be dated early in the history of the building or late? Finally, how are we to interpret these three plastered floors?

The excavators' answer is clear. First, Room 1 existed before the walls that define Courtyard 5-6 were built. Pavement B is to be associated with the walls of Room 1 and confirms its existence in the Early Roman period. However, within the first century three floors were laid down above Pavement B. These floors are all plastered and contain tiny fragments of Herodian lamps but lack kitchenware. Finally, there are many fragments of plaster with inscriptions of the second and third centuries that fell down within the walls when this room was converted into a house-church in the fourth century.[19]

In other words, the excavators conclude that the house was founded about 100 B.C.E. Sometime near the end of the first century C.E., someone plastered it three times, which may suggest conversion to a public building rather than merely the remodeling of a house. (At Capernaum, stone pavements are the rule for houses.) Furthermore, the absence of plain pottery correlates with a public rather than a private use for this part of the building. Finally, since pilgrims were incising graffiti of Christian character on the plastered walls of Room 1 in the second and third centuries, it is reasonable to conclude that the Christian community had converted this room into a house-church (*domus-ecclesia*) with the renovations of the plastered floors and walls.

The critic will be quick to point out that such evidence is circumstantial and slim. After all, it is not impossible that a wealthy family turned to plaster as a symbol of status. Also, a report on the "tiniest fragments of Herodian lamps . . . collected in the thin layers of the plaster pavement" needs to be published, at least in part, to determine if they are early- or late-type Herodian lamps.[20] The late type is known in the second century c.e.. The one intact Herodian lamp from this level and the single base that are published are early types, but we need more data.[21] Though one may insist that the evidence as reported is necessary to the excavators' conclusion (that this is indeed Peter's house and was venerated continuously until the fourth century), it is not sufficient. As formulated, this conclusion is really a working hypothesis to be tested with further excavation. Perhaps future investigations will provide even more unambiguous evidence for the student and historian. In the meantime we have, provisionally speaking, the oldest Christian sanctuary unearthed anywhere.

We have spoken earlier of the finds at Nazareth.[22] It would be instructive now to examine the archaeological evidence for another possible early Christian edifice there that is in some ways analogous to the site of Capernaum.

Nazareth

Beneath the imposing Basilica of the Annunciation at Nazareth are remains suggestive of early Christian veneration of the site.[23] These include a small cave beneath the north aisle of a fifth-century Byzantine church and a ritual bath, or *mikveh*, beneath the nave of the same church. The south stylobate of this church was discovered to be a preexisting wall simply reused. Other fragments of walls from a pre-Byzantine structure did not escape the archaeologist's spade.

The Byzantine church is oriented east to west, as all churches ordinarily were. Interestingly enough, the fragment of mosaic floor in the nave is oriented to the north. It contained a large cross in a wreath. The craftsman worked the Greek letter *rho* into this equal-armed cross, suggestive of a Chi-Rho monogram. This mosaic fragment is 5.3 by 2.0

meters and appears to date to the fourth century. Therefore it antedated the building of the church.[24]

Directly north of this fragment of mosaic, six rock-cut steps lead down to a small cave of three chambers.[25] The floor of the first chamber of the cave is about 1.25 meters below the level of the mosaic in the nave. This chamber is paved with a mosaic about 2.95 meters north to south. To the east it is now destroyed after approximately 3.0 meters, so its original extent can no longer be deduced. Judging from the cuttings in bedrock it seems likely that it did not exceed 6 meters. This mosaic contains an inscription: "Offering of Conon, Deacon of Jerusalem."[26] It is worth noting that the first word (offering), abbreviated in the text, is the word that is used in Romans 15:16 and is common elsewhere in Jewish literature. The excavators assume that this Conon is a namesake of the famous martyr of Nazareth killed under Decius (249–251) in Pamphylia in Asia Minor. In court he is reported to have said, "I am of the city of Nazareth in Galilee, I am of the family of Christ, to whom I offer a cult from the time of my ancestors."[27]

Due north of the inscription of Conon is a small cave, pointed at the back. It measures only 4.7 by 2.3 meters. Masons plastered its walls no less than six times in antiquity. Since the third coat of plaster included a coin of the young, beardless Constantine, plasterings one and two must have antedated the fourth century, though how much it is difficult to say. The earliest plaster includes an inscription painted in red (a *dipinto*) that seems to be a petition to "Christ Lord" to "save thy servant Valeria."[23] The rest is fragmented. The excavator thinks the inscription dates to the "early Christian centuries." The shapes of the letters lead one to conclude that the inscription is third century.

Northeast of the Conon mosaic is yet another cave, this one provided with a rock-cut apse at its east end. The previous small cave is called the "martyrium," because the excavators believed it commemorated the martyrdom of Conon of Nazareth in the third century. This larger cave is called "the

Grotto of the Annunciation," for local tradition associates it with the events of Luke 1:26-38. Its measurements are 5.50 by 6.14 meters. Nothing in the cave is datable. The existence of this cave and others does suggest to us, however, that early churches tended to be erected over small caves.[29]

Let us return to the mosaic fragment in the middle of the nave of the Byzantine church. When this mosaic was lifted, the excavators discovered that this mosaic fragment partially covered an ancient basin, probably a ritual bath (*mikveh*).[30] Its builders cut it out of the bedrock as a cube two meters on a side. A set of seven steps led down westward into the bath on its south side. It is clear that the stonemasons who cut the basin were careful to construct seven steps. Five of them they cut from the living rock, while the top two they built of stones and mortar. The northeast corner they outfitted with a quarter-round sump to gather the remnants of the water.[31]

This *mikveh* stands very close to a preexisting wall, that is, one that antedates the Byzantine church. The wall was reused as the south stylobate of the church, but its original function is not yet obvious. The ritual bath is not oriented with either the later Byzantine church or the wall reused as the church's stylobate. It is about 11–12 degrees out of orientation with the stylobate wall. This suggests that it was built neither for the fifth-century church nor for the fourth-century structure next to it. In any case, the mosaic overlying the basin excludes its association with the church.

This basin has no sure indication that it was used as a Jewish-Christian cultic bath. In its fill excavators found many pieces of plaster with graffiti scratched into them. The plaster is painted red, green, and brown, and evidently fell from the walls of the building that were used as the stylobate of the fifth-century church. These graffiti include fragments of words in Greek and Syriac. One Greek graffito *may* be read "Lord Christ," but a *K* is superimposed over an *X*, which is an otherwise unattested abbreviation. The Syriac reads "John," "Amun," and "Mary."[32] We will return to the ritual bath shortly. For the moment, let us confine our attention to the edifice with painted plaster that predated the fifth-century church. What was it?

Just south of the Byzantine church was a contemporary Byzantine convent.[33] In the fill of Room I, sealed beneath Mosaic Fragment 9, excavators recovered many fragments of painted plaster similar to those in the basin. Thirteen coins were too corroded to identify with confidence, but they seem to date to the late fourth or early fifth century C.E. This is in keeping with the date of the fill beneath the floors of the church, except for the central mosaic fragment. Many pieces of polished marble a centimeter thick turned up also in this fill, which suggests that parts of the earlier building were faced with marble. The surprise for the excavators concerns seventy architectural fragments, most probably from this earlier building.[34]

These fragments include five bases, several column drums, and two capitals. In addition, the excavators uncovered three blocks that formed the abutments of double arches with carefully cut moldings. These and other moldings and the column pieces most closely resemble those from the synagogues of the Galilee and Golan heights. Those that have been excavated stratigraphically usually are discovered to have had their founding about mid-third century C.E.

Again it is no more than a testable hypothesis, but these fragments may be most simply interpreted as remnants of a synagogue of the third and fourth centuries C.E. Either the builders of the church dismantled the synagogue, or earthquakes destroyed it in the late fourth or early fifth century C.E. The community erected a church on its site afterward. Some elements of the synagogue they reused in the church, notably the wall that became the south stylobate.

Some of these architectural fragments were plastered, usually a characteristic of Byzantine architecture. Again we encounter graffiti scratched onto these stones. Most are in Greek, but at least two are in Armenian, which is unprecedented. The graffiti are mostly names and otherwise too fragmentary to read, but one must be read either of two ways, both of which seem to be Christian:

Christil, **Hail,**

or

Maria **Maria**

The first word is abbreviated *XE* with a bar above, which is almost always read as an abbreviation for Christ, but since "Jesus" does not appear as a second word, the excavators understand it to be "Hail" and therefore an early attestation to the cult of Mary.[35]

First let us sum up briefly the occupational sequence we are describing, then something of its religious and cultural nature. We have been speaking of a ritual bath that was in use at this spot probably as late as the first half of the third century C.E., although the date of its founding now escapes us. Sometime later in the third century C.E. the community founded a synagogue above it. Contemporary with or earlier than the founding of the synagogue, Christians were probably worshiping in the declivities in the bedrock, perhaps as remnants of a local cult. In the course of the third and fourth centuries, pilgrims came to the cave and to the synagogue and scratched graffiti within the caves. The multiple plasterings inside these grottoes testify to the intensity of visitation. Late in the history of the synagogue some of its stones were plastered, perhaps as a remodeling. Now pilgrims scratched not only their names but also prayers of a Christian character, even on the stones of the synagogue.

That there should be a synagogue but no church should not surprise us, for Midrash Ecclesiastes 2:8 speaks of priestly families in Nazareth in the early third century. Even Epiphanius as late as 377 C.E. says the town is wholly Jewish, evidently meaning that no citizens of non-Jewish extraction were to be found there.

Egeria came through Nazareth between 381 and 384. Her comments are used by Peter and the Deacon in 1193, and the sentence that mentions the synagogue could well be hers, though it may come from a later source:

> There is a big and very splendid cave in which she [that is, Holy Mary] lived. An altar has been placed there, and there, within the actual cave, is the place from which she drew water. Inside the city the synagogue where the Lord read the book of Isaiah is now a church, but the spring from which Holy Mary used to take water is outside the village.[36]

There is some confusion in the sources, for there is no spring inside the cave. This reference must be to the cave and spring in the present Church of Saint Gabriel. The spring was inside the early village, but the boundary was moved by the twelfth century, which accounts for Peter's belief that it is "now" outside the church.[37]

Somewhere after the middle of the fourth century the mosaics were built in the synagogue, but oriented north, and also inside the caves. The last three coats of plaster inside the martyrium appeared at this time. Since the mosaics include crosses, it seems inescapable that the synagogue had by then become a church.

At the end of the fourth century and beginning of the fifth, the synagogue was either destroyed (perhaps by the severe earthquake of 419[38]) or simply dismantled. In its place the Christian community built a small church that reused at least one wall of the synagogue. The nave of the church covered exactly the area associated with the caves and the ritual bath, though the specific memory of the bath may already have been lost. This church is likely the one seen by the Pilgrim of Piacenza about 570. Just to the south of the church was an attached monastery or convent, beneath whose pavement the excavators found the building blocks and other architectural fragments of the synagogue.

The mosaic contains simple rectangles outlined in black against a white background. In the bottom of the basin there is another pattern of five rectangles in a line, parallel to the steps, with another rectangle at the end on the west.

It may be that both these ritual baths were actually early Jewish-Christian baptistries, as E. Testa has suggested.[41] This is possible, but remains speculative. More apposite is simply that the two churches that cover the earliest remains in Nazareth conceal similar earlier cultic installations on the same orientation. Also, their occupational histories appear to be the same. Unfortunately, the cave and *mikveh* beneath the Church of Saint Joseph have no graffiti to suggest an early Christian veneration. Also, the excavations of 1890 and 1909–10 were not controlled enough either in the *mikveh* or in the artificial cave to give us much more evidence.[42]

Caves and the Christian Tradition

It must not escape us that worship in caves is already a strongly attested tradition in the fourth century and that we can find precedents in the third. As a matter of fact, literary references to caves associated with Christian traditions can be found here and there, alerting us to the possibility that such sites may have been endemic to certain types of early Christian worship. The birth of Jesus is located in a cave according to the Papyrus Bodmer V "Birth of Mary; Revelation of James," otherwise known as the Protevangelium of James (18:1):[43]

And he [Joseph] found a cave there and brought her into it, and left her in the care of his sons, and went out to seek for a Hebrew midwife in the region of Bethlehem.

It is significant that many early churches are built over caves: the Eleona in Jerusalem, as well as the Church of the Holy Sepulchre and the Church of the Nativity in Bethlehem.

Other caves are mentioned in ancient Christian literature.[44]

Benoit and Boismard have published a chance find of a likely third- or early fourth-century Christian holy cave from Bethany.[45] In its first use it had been a cistern about 3.20 meters deep approached from the west side by a stairway and door. A broad set of five steps across the 5.4-meter width allowed those who fetched water to dip out the last liter from the lowest end on the east. In the late third or early fourth century, a Christian community transformed this cistern into a cave-sanctuary. At this point they coated the inside walls and floor with a bluish coat of plaster containing ash.

The excavators found this plaster covered with no less than seventy-one graffiti in Greek (sixty-seven examples), Latin (two examples), Syriac (one example), and Syriac or Arabic (one). In the opinion of the excavators, the earliest graffito (no. 43) must be from about the fourth century. It reads: "God of the Christians, have mercy on the sinner Anamos and remit him his sins." Anamos is a Palmyrene or Nabataean name. The other names are Greek, Arabic, Aramaic, and perhaps Syriac in origin. Many crosses also adorn the walls, some of them the Constantinian monogram type.[46]

Thus, though the remains are scanty and difficult to interpret, we can indeed detect early Christian sanctuaries in Palestine. Only one of them may be of the first century, and in this case its public character is given away by the simple plastering of the floors and walls of one large room of a house. There is a chance, therefore, that other early Christian sanctuaries exist in other places, particularly in houses mentioned in the New Testament. These would include the houses of the apostles' gathering in Jerusalem (Acts 2:1, etc.), the house of Cornelius at Caesarea (Acts 10:1ff), and various other places.

Perhaps more interesting as examples of folk religion are the caves to be found here and there, generally beneath fourth-century churches. That this mode of worship is not entirely orthodox is implied by the fulminations of Cyril, preaching in Jerusalem in mid-fourth century.

> When you find yourself a stranger in any city, do not ask for the "House of God," for the sects of the impious also give this name to their caves. Nor ask either, "Where is the church?", but specify well and ask for the *Catholic* Church. (Migne, *Patrologiae Graeca* 33.1047-8)

Finally, we have mentioned the use, or even building, of synagogues by the followers of Jesus, as is indicated by the finds in Nazareth. This should also be of no particular surprise, for the Epistle of James in the New Testament addressed itself to the problem of discrimination by wealth on the part of Christians when visitors entered "your [synagogue]" (James 2:2). It is important to notice that the pattern emerging is one of diversity. We should not expect that archaeological evidence or, for that matter, literary evidence will all point to one practice. The early followers of Jesus frequented the temple, synagogues, and assemblies in houses. It is certainly within the bounds of reason that many of them participated in local cults, as at Mamre and elsewhere, which may help account for their interest in caves. Therefore, to use rather awkward, later terminology, we expect to find more house-churches, synagogue-churches, and cave-churches within the limits of Eretz Israel.

139

7

Synagogues,
Art, and the
World of the Sages

Surprising as it may seem, it is only fairly recently that evidence for "early" synagogues of the first centuries C.E. has come to light. Although previous generations of scholars assumed the existence of distinct physical structures in this period, documentation for them was virtually nonexistent. To be sure, literary as well as epigraphic support[1] for supposing such a reality was always great, and only the excavations which produced the first-century-C.E. prayer houses at Masada, Herodium, Magdala (Tarichaeae), and Gamala have necessitated a reevaluation of the question of how and where Jews prayed during this formative period. While Herodium and Masada might be understood to represent only a limited strata of society, one in close relationship with Jerusalem royalty, Magdala on the western shore of the Sea of Galilee and Gamala in the Golan reveal edifices created by thriving rural communities quite independent of the royal house.[2]

Both Josephus and a contemporary scholar number the synagogues of first-century Jerusalem in the hundreds,[3] but apart from the Theodotus inscription discussed earlier, there is virtually no archaeological trace of them. What we have in this instance is a problem of terminology that needs clarification both here and in scholarly literature. Although the Greek term *synagogue* connotes a place of assembly, as does its Semitic equivalent *beth knesset,* it sheds no light whatever on the physical nature of what was thought to be such an assembly place.[4] The primary functions of a synagogue were prayer and study, hence the terms *beth tefilah* (house of prayer) or *beth midrash* (house of study).[5] It is highly likely, therefore, that in the period when the Temple still stood, a synagogue could well have been nothing more than a large meeting room in a private house or part of a larger structure set apart for worship. If this were the case, then the argument for house-churches at Capernaum and elsewhere becomes all the more compelling.

When the Jewish population of Judaea and Samaria began to establish themselves in Galilee after the Roman wars, one of the first problems was the issue of how and where to pray. On the basis of archaeological evidence from more than one hundred ancient Palestinian synagogues, however, it is difficult to date the earliest evidences of synagogues before the mid-third century C.E. The import of this data is quite clear, namely, it took a century or more for these newly established communities to accumulate sufficient means to build public places of worship in which they invested not only considerable funds but even more their hopes and wishes for a better future in the richly variegated architectural monuments of the talmudic period.

In recent years, the bulk of scholarly effort on the subject of ancient synagogues has been devoted to new excavations and to the study of architectural development. Indeed, new evidence is now so abundant that a period of reevaluation has set in, in order to assess the data that has become available since the Six-Day War of 1967. While it may be said that the American effort in this field has been devoted toward establishing a group of datable buildings so that a reassessment might be possible, a derivative aspect of their work has been recognition of the surprising variety in Palestinian synagogues, a fact that had not been recognized prior to the

141

excavations at Khirbet Shema' during 1970–72.[6] Both these factors have led us to reexamine prior assumptions. The mere fact of being unleashed from the fetters of older typological views on the development of the synagogue as a distinct architectural reality has enabled us to ask questions in the social-historical realm which would have been unthinkable a decade ago.

Several seminal works on talmudic archaeology still dominate the field and collect the many literary sources for understanding the furnishings and the terminology of the synagogue.[7] What needs to be done today is to relate such studies to excavated remains which are fully published and for which a consensus about dating exists. The recent furor over the late chronology of the synagogue at Capernaum only underscores how disagreements over chronology and raw data interfere with the more synthetic task of social-historical reconstruction.[8] If one accepts the analysis of the house-church offered in the previous chapter and at the same time a late chronology for the synagogue at Capernaum, then there begins to emerge a picture of religious diversity and pluralism that needs to be more fully explored. It would appear that at this pilgrim center on the northwest corner of Lake Kinnereth, Jews, Jewish-Christians, and Christians all might have lived together, the new wealth of the fourth century enabling the major building effort to occur as Palestine became more and more a center for tourists with its elevated status to Holy Land now a reality.

The Variety and Chronology of Palestinian Synagogue Buildings

The Basilica

Excluding any consideration of the four early synagogues mentioned above, and presupposing a period of major regrouping and population movement from south to north after 70 c.e. and 135 c.e., we have organized the present discussion by types of synagogues without assuming any typological development whatever. The basilica, perhaps the most familiar type to most readers, is characterized by an elaborate triple-portal facade which faces south toward Jerusalem. The floor of such a structure is thought to have been paved with simple stone slabs. Its ground plan is "basilical," with two rows of columns running north-south and often a transverse row closing the shorter northern side. Space is accordingly divided into a central nave and two side aisles. An upper story or gallery is usually assumed to have existed along these three rows, though it is a matter of some dispute whether it was used exclusively for women in the ancient period.[9] Furthermore, the very existence of a second story is undergoing scrutiny today. The excavators of Capernaum, for example, are now convinced that there was no gallery at Capernaum whatever and that a simple shed roof was carried by a total column height—from base to capital—of five meters.

In addition to the above-mentioned features, stone benches were often provided for worshipers along the sides. It might be conjectured, however, that many worshipers simply sat on the floor as is customary to this day in a mosque, because there is never sufficient bench space provided to utilize effectively most of the interior space.

In the basilica, as in the variant forms of the ancient synagogue, the major architectural, if not theological, concern is the wall of orientation which always faces Jerusalem. It is generally assumed that this most salient and telling feature of the synagogue is derived from the biblical practice of praying toward Jerusalem (I Kings 8:44, par. II Chron. 6:34; I Kings 8:48, par. II Chron. 6:38; Dan. 6:10). This custom achieves legal force in the rabbinic period when it is translated into law (*y. Berakot* 4. 8*b–c*), but the same principle seems to have been operative in the first-century buildings at Masada and Herodium.[10]

The principle of sacred orientation may be observed in the basilical structure found in the American excavations at ancient Meiron, where the triple facade faces south toward Jerusalem.[11] It has hitherto been assumed that in a basilical synagogue of this kind the ark was not yet a permanent fixture but a portable structure wheeled out during worship into the main sanctuary. The precentor, or reader, of Scripture would stand before it facing Jerusalem. Possible representations of the portable ark may be observed in sculpture at Capernaum and in mosaic elsewhere.[12] In our view, the portable ark of the synagogue harks back to Nathan's rebuke of David (II Sam. 7:4ff.), when the prophet argued poignantly in theological terms for a movable shrine.

Both the orientation of the basilica and the suggested location of the ark require the so-called awkward about-face of the worshiper. That is, if the Jerusalem entrances were both functional and used as the focus of worship, the worshiper would have to turn around immediately after entering the building from the south. The lack of an entryway on the northern, or opposite, side necessitates such a turnaround. At Meiron, as well as most other basilical sites, no convincing proof of entrances on the north, east, or west has yet been found.

All this presupposes the existence of a Torah shrine on the interior southern, or Jerusalem-facing, wall, and even though none has been found *in situ,* the evidence at both Meiron and Capernaum supports such a theory.[13] At Beth She' arim, a novel arrangement is found in the basilicalike synagogue excavated there: a raised *bema* (podium) is situated in the back wall of the nave opposite the three monumental doorways that face toward Jerusalem. The building dates from the second quarter of the third century to the middle of the fourth century.[14]

If the Torah shrine was portable, then we would not expect to find a trace of it.[15] The excavators at Beth She' arim, however, note a significant change toward the last phase of the building's history when a Torah shrine is relocated on the Jerusalem wall. The excavator of the En-gedi synagogue has also observed a similar shift.[16] Both instances tend to suggest a major theological development sometime in the late third or early fourth century C.E., when public reading of Scripture in a worship setting reached a genuine high point. Whether or not such a shift can be related to circumstances affecting the Jewish community, such as the Christianization of the empire by Constantine or the reading of Scripture by sectarians, is a matter that deserves further study.

The origin of the basilica style is generally conceded to be the typical Greco-Roman basilica, possibly mediated to Palestine through builders employed by Herod the Great. Herod was himself one of the most notable patrons of Roman building in the entire Eastern Mediterranean world. Still others would suggest that the basilica was mediated through Syro-Roman and Nabataean prototypes. In any case, the synagogue *qua* basilica is still innovative in the sense that a public structure which emphasized the exterior has been modified to suit unique religious purposes.

We may summarize the "older" views on the development of the synagogue, best exemplified in the writings of Avi-Yonah, in the following manner: (1) The Galilean, or basilical, synogogue is the oldest of Palestinian synagogues. (2) The broadhouse represents a transitional phase in its development and reflects a time when efforts were expended to fix a permanent place for the ark. (3) The apsidal building is the final stage of development, in which the worshiper enters opposite the orienting wall and faces the sacred Torah shrine directly. Basically, such an evolutionary theory presupposed a certain chronology that can no longer be maintained.

New discoveries now indicate a much higher degree of flexibility in dating these types and attest the simultaneous existence of one type alongside another. Capernaum, for example, is widely regarded as late, or Byzantine, whereas Khirbet Shema' is early. It is our contention that the only certain way of dating any ancient building is through scientific excavation and scholarly evaluation of the data which emanates from such excavation. With respect to the general categories of synagogue buildings, in addition to the divergencies in ground plan and internal furnishings already mentioned, present excavations reveal even further anomalies so that even the concept of a standard basilica cannot be maintained any longer.

The American excavations in 1977 and 1978 at the ancient site of Gush Halav (Gischala), just a few kilometers north of Meiron, reinforce the opinion already stated that only careful excavation can provide the answers to serious questions of dating and typology.[17] In the jargon of field archaeologists, this site provides a classic example of the axiom that "the answers always lie below." In the case of Kohl and Watzinger, who excavated at Gush Halav during their survey in the early part of this century, they clearly did not go deep enough in their work. Their published plan of Gush Halav indicates that they erroneously took what are now clearly storage areas as the closing or interior wall of a very large square basilica.[18] Our work at Gush Halav demonstrates the errors in the German typological assumptions and supports the notion that variety exists even within the broadly defined category of "basilical synagogues."

To be sure, the founding of the Gush Halav synagogue can be dated to the third century c.e., but the southern wall that faces Jerusalem has only one entrance, namely, the one with the down-facing eagle incised on the underside of its lintel stone. If a gallery for additional seating existed, it would have been on the northern side, where the only other certain entrance to the building has been found. What is basilical about this building is its two rows of four columns running north-south. It is rectangular only if we take its newly discovered interior load-bearing walls as defining the interior space of the building. Indeed, the interest of this building lies in the fact that these interior walls, on the west, north, and east, demarcate the interior space of the building and transform a roughly square structure—originally thought by the Germans to be the synagogue interior—into a rectangular basilica internally. That is to say, we must place a large corridor on the western side, a gallery on the north, and a series of rooms along the eastern side, which is a unique arrangement for a "basilica synagogue."

Of major interest also is the *bema*, or podium, for the reading of scrolls, discovered along the southern wall, which happens to be the only ashlar wall among all the exterior walls. The *bema* dates to the fourth century or second phase of the building's use and is off center in the building, just to the west of the sole entrance on the south wall facing Jerusalem. Among the debris, however, were smaller pieces of architectural fragments that suggest an *aedicula*, or Torah shrine, in conjunction with this *bema*—possibly built atop it—or in still another phase. The discovery of the *bema* at Gush Halav represents the first of its kind in the general category of buildings we call basilical, save for the anomalous situations we noted at Beth She' arim and En-gedi.

New data brings new insights. While the material from Gush Halav alters somewhat the older views, it underscores the capacity of an individual religious community for originality within certain parameters. The overall architectural forms, however immersed within the Greco-Roman provincial world they may be, reflect a looseness and freedom from rigidity that is refreshing to the student of Roman provincial art.

The Broadhouse

The broadhouse synagogue receives its designation because its wall of orientation is one of the longer or broader walls, as opposed to the shorter endwall in the basilica. Despite the fact that the oldest known example of this type comes from Dura-Europos and dates from the first half of the third century C.E., in Palestine the broadhouse synagogue was traditionally thought to be late (fourth century C.E.) and transitional, that is, between the Roman basilica discussed above and the Byzantine apsidal synagogue. In general, its appearance seems to coincide with a time when a fixed receptacle for the Torah was adopted. Among the known broadhouse synagogues the *bema* is the most widely attested feature, and it is always situated on the wall oriented toward Jerusalem. The broadhouse represents one solution to the awkward about-face required by the basilica, for in this instance one can as easily enter via a short wall and face the Torah shrine as one can enter via the long wall opposite the shrine. It may simply represent an independent predilection for an architectural type which already had a lengthy history in ancient Palestine. Both types find resolution in the first and only Galilean broadhouse excavated, at Khirbet Shema', just one kilometer south of ancient Meiron. As indicated above, other scholars have understood such a building to be the result of architectural adjustments made to accommodate the new emphasis on Scripture in worship and the concomitant addition of a Torah shrine.[19]

The conclusive dating of two major phases of the Khirbet Shema' broadhouse synagogue to the third and fourth centuries C.E. once again forces students of ancient synagogues to put aside preconceived developmental notions of stages in their history and study the evidence alone. Khirbet Shema', while clearly a broadhouse, with orientation in both stages on the long south wall, differs from its closest parallels at Susiyeh and Eshtemoa in Judaea by having internal columnation running east-west, ninety degrees off the wall oriented toward Jerusalem. None of the other broadhouse synagogues excavated to date has supporting columns in the sacred area, rather, they use radically widened walls to support their superstructure.

It should be underscored that the dates arrived at in this discussion for the phases and salient features of the synagogues at Khiret Shema', Gush Halav, and Meiron are based upon the chronological data provided by "critical loci" recovered during excavation. In every case these dates synchronize well with the chronological data recovered from the rest of the site. They are the results of careful consideration of all ceramic and numismatic materials, in conjunction with geological information available about ancient earthquake patterns in Upper Galilee.

The three sites which have been excavated and studied by the authors and the Meiron Excavation Project team all lie in a region of intense earthquake activity from ancient times until the present. In fact, the Safed-Gush Halav-Meiron area constitutes a major fault line in the Safed epicenter.[20] While this reality has created untold damage and suffering through the years, it has in many ways made the archaeological task somewhat easier. At Khirbet Shema' we were able to conclude that the first synagogue building of the second half of the third century C.E. was completely destroyed in the great earthquake of 306 C.E. The evidence for the destruction of Synagogue I at Khirbet Shema' emerged dramatically in the course of excavations beneath the floor in the east end of the second or post-306 building; here were recovered fragments of columns, capitals, and bases, all shattered so badly that they could be used only as rubble building material, or fill.

The destruction date of the second Shema' building can be arrived at with some ease because there is a sharp break in the coin evidence after 408 C.E. Since most fifth-century coins were produced under Arcadius and Honorius early in the century, and hence later specimens would not normally be expected, the best explanation for such a radical break in the coin profile is a sudden abandonment of the site. This is further corroborated by the tumbled and badly shattered debris of Synagogue II. Dating by the closest "strong earthquake" after 408 C.E., it is possible to conclude that the occupation of the entire site—comparing all the data from the entire town—came to an abrupt end in the earthquake of 419 C E. Scientists of the Geologic Survey of Israel, who have just concluded a long-range study of the Upper Galilee region, have studied the pictures of the destroyed *in situ* remains in Synagogue II and were able to confirm the direction of the ancient fall, which was determined by the fault lines recently plotted by them. Their study has also corroborated the direction of the Gush Halav collapse and has enabled us to explain the extensive repairs done at Meiron in the first half of the fourth century C.E.

In sectioning, or cutting through, the *bema* at Khirbet Shema', we were fortunate enough to recover a number of coins which enabled us to conclude that the people at Khirbet Shema' did not wait long to rebuild their sacred sanctuary but attempted to reestablish their lives immediately. Since the rubble-filled *bema* dates to after 306, and because an earlier bench runs through it and along the southern wall, it may be concluded that in the third-century building there was no *bema*. Fractured remains of smaller architectural elements, however, suggest that a Torah shrine probably stood on this wall in the first structure.

The origin of the broadhouse, therefore, need not be sought at Dura, in our opinion, but may be viewed rather as being descendant from the basic Syro-Palestinian broadhouse temple. In the case of Khirbet Shema', we apparently have a "mixed" type, a kind of merger between the Roman basilica (viewing the building east-west with its two rows of four columns) and the Syro-Palestinian broadhouse (viewing the building along the long southern orienting wall). In any event, it represents a novel adaptation of existing prototypes and gives ample testimony to the ingenuity of the designers.

The Apsidal Synagogue

The third general category of synagogue building is the apsidal structure, clearly the latest of all types—judging from attested remains and inscriptions—with a basilican interior. Dating to the fifth century C.E. and continuing until the eighth century, the novelty of the apsidal synagogue lies in the fact that the apse points in the direction of Jerusalem and constitutes the focus of worship. It represents another solution to the awkwardness of the basilical arrangements described above by enabling the worshiper to face directly in the sacred direction when entering from the east or any side opposite the Jerusalem wall. In this type of structure the apse is usually separated by a screen from the rest of the sanctuary and often serves as the repository for the Torah shrine and possibly also for the storage of old scrolls.

In many buildings there is a platform (*bema*) within the apse, suggestive of the place where the reader or precentor stood, along with the cantor (or *hazzan*), translators, and elders. In this regard it is functionally equivalent to the *bema* at Khirbet Shema' or Gush Halav, though in those places there is only room for the reader of Scripture or *hazzan* (*t. Sukka* 4.6 and pars.). The apsidal building provides the best possible arrangement for explaining the rabbinic mention of the elders sitting with their *backs* toward Jerusalem, that is, to the orienting wall (*t.Megilla* 4.21). According to this same rabbinic source, the only other time leaders turned their backs to Jerusalem was during the recitation of the priestly blessing by the priests themselves.

In the apsidal structure, perhaps because of strictures against the building of new synagogues by the Byzantines, even limiting repairs to points of breach, emphasis is now shifted from the exterior to the interior. This shift in emphasis, if indeed such a datum be accepted, is usually observed in the colorful and richly decorated mosaics that adorn the floors. There mosaics often consist of depictions of biblical episodes but sometimes present borrowed Greek themes as well, such as the signs of the zodiac (Hammath Tiberias, Beth Shean, and others). Often, too, the mosaic directly in front of the apse represents the Torah shrine flanked by the seven-branched candelabra (Beth Alpha). A good example of the apsidal synagogue may be found at Ma'on, Jericho and Gaza, Beth

Alpha, Hammath, Tiberias (last phase), and Hammath Gader.

In summary, then, one might characterize the state of synagogue studies as being in flux. The mass of new material has created a healthy climate for reconsideration and reevaluation. To be sure, many of the old theories have foundered, but that is how those who put them forward would have it. While there is no longer a typological approach to this subject, the old types still persist. Today, however, they persist in startling new variety. When all the new data is ultimately published, it is certain we will know far more about the working of the ancient synagogue than ever before, and archaeology will surely continue to provide a rich source for supplementing the literary record. The point on which the literary and nonliterary records merge is the role of Scripture in ancient worship. Surely further study and more excavation will continue to document this particular aspect of ancient civilization.

Art and the World of the Sages

We have noted in chapter 2 as well as in the preceding section that regional factors have greatly affected the kind of art attested in the synagogues of late antiquity. At the same time, it is evident that by the third and fourth centuries a more lenient attitude of the rabbis can be documented in the sources, an apparent relaxation of the stricter interpretation that some sages gave to the second commandment (Exod. 20:4; Deut. 5:8). This tendency had been noted long ago by Samuel Krauss, who underscored the significance of the targumist Pseudo-Jonathan's comment on Lev. 26:1: "A stone ornamented with pictures you shall not place in your land to bow down upon it. However, a stone on which figures and likenesses are carved you may put on the floors of your sanctuaries, but not to prostrate yourselves on it."[21] This liberalizing attitude may also be documented in the period of

152

Rabbi Johanan bar Nappaha, the third-century sage, during whose life the Talmud says the sages "began to have paintings on the walls, and the rabbis did not forbid" (y. *Aboda Zara* 3.3.1). And a Leningrad fragment of the Palestinian Talmud refers to the mosaics in the days of Rabbi Abun who "did not hinder" his contemporaries from designing them [22] Rabbi Abun lived in the first half of the fourth century C.E.

From those few references alone, not to mention many others, it may be concluded in the light of the evidence from Jewish catacombs at Beth She' arim and from synagogue art that a good portion of rabbinic leadership in the talmudic period saw no conflict between representational art and Jewish learning. That some rabbis did, however, is evidenced by the defacing of images at many sites. The extent to which such leniency with regard to art represents an accommodation to Hellenism may be resolved by our analysis of the clustering of such art remains in the Rift Valley and urban centers of antiquity. A growing flirtation with mysticism and astrology, well-documented in the rabbinic literature, may also account for this kind of flexibility. But it is surely not necessary to conclude, as Goodenough did, that such art was inspired by a kind of illicit mysticism not sanctioned by rabbinic authorities.

The real question yet to be sufficiently addressed is the meaning of many Greek symbols, such as helios, in Jewish contexts in view of the documentation for a more lenient attitude on the part of the rabbis. There is a growing tendency today to suggest that the decoration of these synagogues or tombs is purely ornamental and devoid of any metahistorical significance.[23] While Goodenough might have overstated his case by claiming it presupposed a mystical subculture, he at least has left some of us to go forward in trying to comprehend the meaning of Jewish representational art. Studies in the mural paintings of the third-century synagogue of Dura-Europos, suggested by some to be approved by Rabbi Johanan bar Nappaha, leave open the possibility that narrative art and figural representation have a still earlier history in Palestine that is unknown to us. At the very least, we urge the reader to remain open to the possibility that the issue of Jewish art is still open-ended and requires much further study. The absence of such art in the rural setting of Upper Galilee forces upon us the recognition that segments of the population more conservative than others might have chosen quite intentionally to live in one region and not another. Another factor too is the ambience of the great cities of antiquity, spurned by many as representing a true threat to the preservation of religion.

The second commandment could well have constituted a watershed in the history of Judaism, and it is incumbent upon all students of that history to consider the import of the extreme differences between a Khirbet Shema' on the one hand and a Hammath Tiberias on the other.

8

Jewish and Christian Attachment to Palestine

The Place of Eretz Israel in Rabbinic Theology

Recent scholarship has made little effort to evaluate the widely held view that the Jewish notion of the primacy of the "land of Israel" was declining by late antiquity. The centrality of the doctrines of the land as sacred center and as a reality to be achieved by the pilgrim in life or death has been given only minor consideration by scholars. One of the reasons for this situation is that the notion of the land itself does not lend itself to convenient theological categories or comport well with modern views of universalism.

A major exception to this situation is provided by the grandiose treatment of the territorial doctrine of the land by W. D. Davies.[1] While *The Gospel and the Land* succeeds in espousing the Jewish attachment to the land in biblical and early rabbinic times, it does not go beyond the first century of the common era in its treatment. In fact, the last portion of the work is devoted entirely to the "early" Christian transformation of Israel's doctrine of the land. Davies' work has inspired much of the thinking in this present chapter, though we regret his decision to end his work so early in the Roman period. It is in the tannaitic period especially that a renewed sense of the importance of the land achieves its most poignant articulation in rabbinic Judaism, and it is in post-Constantinian Christianity that the idea of "holy land" comes to play so central a role in the church.[2] The massive evidence of Christian pilgrimage to Israel from the third century C.E. and of church-building from the early fourth century C.E., when viewed together, testifies to the recrudescence of Christian attachment to the land within the early church itself. Even more, however, it suggests the possibility of a Jewish-Christian presence in the Holy Land from the destruction of Jerusalem in C.E. 70 until Constantine.

One reason the present topic has been relegated to discussions of Jewish eschatology and messianism has been the prevalence of the view that after the wars against Rome Judaism was a religon without a homeland, with its major focus in the Diaspora, especially Babylonia, save for its quiet presence in the Holy Land until Byzantine times. To be sure, this is an exaggeration of the historical situation, but nonetheless one which has won broad acceptance.[3] With the documentation of a flourishing Diaspora in Second Temple times, it is quite understandable how one might bypass the place of Eretz Israel in such a context.[4] Also, since students of religion are committed to the presentation of ideas, both Jewish and non-Jewish scholars have often treated the study of Judaism in metaphysical terms alone. As Gerson Cohen has put it: "Accordingly, what place could Palestine, or, for that matter, any particular country have in their system except as a secondary and essentially accidental theme, that is, by virtue of its being the Biblical Holy Land and the messianic land of promise? And so it has been for the most part treated."[5]

Among the legal writings of the Jewish people, however, clearly more than one-third of the law has to do with situations that obtain *only* in the land of Israel (*m. Qiddushin* 1.9). That is to say, the rabbis propound the view that God's dialogue with Israel could not have occurred anywhere but in Israel proper, nor could any other people besides Israel have qualified for such special favor. In the words of the Midrash: "The Holy One, blessed be He, considered all lands, and found no land suitable to be given Israel other than the land of Israel. This is what is meant by the verse 'He rose and measured the earth' (Habakkuk 3:6)."[6] With such an unqualified notion of the centrality of the land in the religion of rabbinic Judaism, it is not surprising that the rabbis, following their biblical forebears, should glorify and exaggerate to a great extent the fecundity of Eretz Israel as a land flowing with "milk and honey" (Exod. 3:3) and avoid the conclusion that Palestine was really a very poor arid region whose climate and topography were anything but desirable for agriculture.

If we were to examine the full range of archaeological data available for the study of rabbinic Judaism, we might well have the impression that the Diaspora communities came to dominate the Jewish world and indeed to outweigh Palestinian Jewry.[7] This is a testimony to the viability of the synagogue as a social and religious institution that it is so well documented, archaeologically speaking, both in Palestine and in the Diaspora during the Roman period. The synagogue more than any other aspect of ancient Judaism enabled the rabbis to transport their faith and to establish it at new places in Palestine and elsewhere. Still, the special superior legal position gained by fulfilling certain commandments in Palestine encouraged pious Jews throughout the ages to "go up to Jerusalem, to *the* Land," as pilgrims discharging a sacred vow.[8] In the Bible, Moses is denied entry into the land, but he is not denied the idiom of family burial (Num. 20:14 ff., 27:12-13; Deut. 1:37, 3:26, 4:21), "to be gathered to his people" in death. The Midrash is as bothered by the anomaly of Moses' death in Transjordan as much as the priestly writer and the Deuteronomist, but a third-century homilist resolves the matter in a predictable way: "Why was Moses our teacher so eager to enter the land of Israel? Was he in need of its fruits or of its bounty? Moses, however, pleaded thus with the Almighty: 'The people of Israel have been given many commandments which can only be fulfilled in the land. Permit me to enter that I too may fulfill them personally.' "[9]

Despite the ascendancy of such halakic views and opinions as this, they did not necessarily lead to the exclusion of strong feelings for the reestablishment of some sort of political entity or, even short of that, a kind of independence from Rome. The revolt under Gallus Caesar in 351 C.E. may well testify to such activity, and the revolt itself has left a considerable imprint on the archaeology of fourth-century Palestine. Most notable of the destructions at this time is the rabbinic necropolis in the settlement of Beth She' arim.[10]

If we take early Jewish prayers as indications of the growing rabbinic articulation of the centrality of the land, then the prayer for the "ingathering of the exiles" is a vivid statement regarding the transitory nature of *galut,* or exile. A Jew prayed thrice daily for messianic redemption at the hands of a Davidide who would gather in from the four corners of the world the exiled of the land.[11] Even though the words express the fervent hope for the restoration of the judges of old, the priests of the temple service, and the Levites to their place of worship, it is fair to say that in such an utterance the Jewish people through the ages ultimately link their destinies both to the people Israel and to the land of Israel. While the messianic-eschatological framework for such a prayer pre-supposes a universalistic outlook, it is clothed in the particularistic language of the history and experience of Israel.

And so it is for the custom of reburial in the Holy Land of the rabbis and of the many simple people who believed in a more literal way that their mortal remains should be in physical contact with holy soil before the end of time. While some scholars have questioned whether the practice of reburying desiccated remains of Jews from the Diaspora began in the Second Temple period, most are agreed that it is an attested phenomenon by 200 C.E.[12] Indeed, the archaeological evidence for reburial at Beth She' arim and Tiberias, in particular, provides a useful context in which to understand the working out of the growing and diverse eschatological speculations of the rabbis.

First and foremost in the development of that custom is the idea that the soil of the land itself has atoning power: "And his land shall make expiation for his people" (Deut. 32:43). In rabbinic terms, "anyone who is buried in Eretz Israel it is as if he were buried under the altar [or throne of glory]."[13] Second, it was further believed by the sages that the dead of Eretz Israel would be the first to be resurrected in the messianic era. Even those who are buried outside Israel will ultimately return for the resurrection, rolling along in underground cavities until they too reach the holy land.[14]

The existence of such a theological schema among the rabbis not only provides a raison d'être for the persistence of secondary burials in the late antique period but also enables us to understand the welter of material remains associated with these reinterments. Rather than suggesting a diminution of the role of the land in Jewish theology at this time both the literary and the archaeological remains indicate a strengthening of ties to the land in a period when the political possibilities for reestablishing formal ties or sovereignty over the Holy Land or Temple had to be diminished. As late as in the days of Emperor Julian (late fourth century), Jews still harbored hopes that the Temple would be rebuilt.

The persistence of these views of the land up until the modern era, despite the absence of realistic hopes for actual political realization of those aims, may be understood in terms of the metahistorical reality they presupposed. Although the anticipated outcome of history was constantly being pushed ahead in characteristic proleptic fashion, the expectation of a better future, of redemption, provided succor to those who believed and awaited the final resolution of history.

It is difficult to imagine that the kind of ideas pertaining to the centrality of the land in Jewish theology did not influence to some degree the sacred-land theology of the early Christian church. The fact that so many of the early church shrines commemorate theophanous events of both testaments is surely significant. Consider the elaborate church on Mount Nebo, where Moses was believed to have glimpsed the land, or the Church of the Nativity at Bethlehem, where Jesus was born. Christians also built a church at Kiriath-Jearim "nine miles from Jerusalem" according to Egeria (L2) commemorating the events of I Samuel 7:1-2 and another at the place of the appearance to Abraham of the three angels, then called Terebinthus, today Ramat el-Khalil. Surely such building activities document a continuity between church and synagogue that should be stressed. Similarly, the burial or reburial of Christian martyrs or of their relics in commemorative churches even seems to suggest a continuity between Jewish and Christian burial customs.[14a]

The Place of the Land in Early Christian Theology

A glance at the topics of papers read by New Testament scholars before national and international professional societies shows us that concern for "the Land," or even for history and geography in the New Testament, is definitely on the wane in contemporary scholarship. The topics of interest appear to be literary, theological, exegetical, and methodological, but they hardly touch on questions of place identification, site description, or any other scholarly research that would give flesh and bone to the material setting of the early Christian movement. The new "social histories" are exceptions to this rule, but even they appear to be based upon research into the literature of early Judaism and of the early Roman Empire.[15]

To be sure, certain strains of early Christian literature reflect a preoccupation with the developing thought of the Christian movement rather than with the external anchors in history and geography. Yet it is, after all, the single most intensely "theological" or "symbolic" treatise in the New Testament, namely, the Gospel of John, that is peppered with side-references to the geography of Palestine.[16] For example, it is this Gospel that preserves the tradition of the healing at the pool "with *five* porches" in Jerusalem (in the Bethesda quarter), yet the author does not seem to exploit this detail as a symbol.[17] Even the reference to "Bethany beyond the Jordan" in John 1:28 appears in a manner that suggests the name is being used historically and topographically rather than symbolically. Specifically, we are told that travel from this Bethany to Cana took two days (John 1:28, 43; 2:1-11), and from there to Bethany near Jerusalem took four days (John 10:40–11:18).[18]

It is again the Fourth Gospel alone that asserts against the Synoptic Gospels that John was baptizing "at Aenon near Salim" (3:23). The author assumes the reader will know that the Aenon in question, with a nondistinctive name ("springs"), is near Salim.[19] Furthermore, Jesus performed his first miracle at "Cana in Galilee," which distinguishes this locality from the Cana near Sidon.[20] It is John who tells us that Nathanael is from this Galilean Cana.

These examples could be multiplied many times and supplemented with examples of lore, customs, and other bits of information known to the author of this Gospel. The point we wish to make, however, is simply that an unprejudiced reading of the Gospel of John seems to suggest that it is in fact based on a historical and geographical tradition, though not one that simply repeats information from the Synoptics. In other words, this Gospel, as well as Matthew, Mark, and Luke, firmly anchors its traditions in the land, not in an ideal, heavenly Israel.[21]

Although we have made our point in historical terms, we must hasten to add that the early Christian writers clearly were not writing handbooks of Palestinian geography and lore. Rather, their major concerns were theological—they were investing their energies in self-definition on the theological plane. They simply presupposed the earthly vision of the early Christian to be focused on Palestine. Consequently, there is a certain legitimacy to the earnest inquiry in New Testament studies after the theological and literary dimensions of the sacred-land tradition. We are simply making a plea that its historical, geographical, and even ethnographic dimensions need not thereby be ignored.

These later dimensions of the tradition are perhaps most visible in terms of what one might call folk religion. By "folk religion" we mean what people may say, do, and believe in spite of what the gradually developing official religion may recognize. For example, it is clear that veneration of the tombs of departed saints was an important element in first-century Judaism.[22] Yet the documents of what one might call official religion are strangely silent on this matter. One cannot glean much on the importance of such holy men's tombs from the Mishnah and Talmud; however, they are not without importance in such a study. Rather, it is the literature of the pseudepigrapha, apocrypha, and Jewish pilgrim texts of the Middle Ages that is rich in this tradition.[23]

That the tombs of the biblical saints play a role even in early Christian literature is attested by the Gospel of Matthew, which contains the passage, "the tombs also were opened, and many bodies of the saints who had fallen asleep were raised, and coming out of the tombs after his resurrection they went into the holy city and appeared to many" (27:52-53). Although in many quarters of critical New Testament scholarship this passage is understood as nonhistorical, we simply wish to point out that a cultural datum must lie behind the theological intent of the author if he expects to communicate.[23a]

The veneration of tombs may well have been an element of folk religion in Christianity also, for the canonical books seem little interested in furthering veneration of holy tombs. Nevertheless, a book such as the *Vitae Prophetarum,* which was composed before 135 C.E., is unmistakably Christian in its present form and clearly regards knowing the locations of the prophets' tombs as a vital part of Christian devotion.[24]

162

This interest continues into the heyday of Christian pilgrimage during the fourth century. For example, an anonymous Pilgrim of Bordeaux (333 c.e.) mentions no fewer than nine holy tombs, only one of which belongs to a New Testament figure, namely, Jesus himself.[25] Egeria mentions six holy tombs or graves, two of which are in the New Testament tradition (Jesus' and Lazarus').[26] Yet the account of her travels in Peter the Deacon (1137) is far more complete, mentioning no fewer than twenty holy tombs, only four of which are of New Testament figures (Jesus, James, the son of the widow of Nain, and John the Baptist).[27]

Of course, after a time the original patterns and rationale for veneration of holy tombs may have been forgotten in Christian thought. As a matter of fact, Egeria does not stop to pray at the tombs of any Old Testament figures, only at the tomb of Jesus. Rather, by her time the interest is in seeing with the eye what the heart believes already, namely, the tomb (at least) of an Old Testament saint.

The land is also where the events of the Gospels and the earlier chapters of the book of Acts took place. Therefore, in a manner analogous to events in ancient Scripture, Christians sought out those places associated with the life of Jesus or the early church. Often this took the form of locating caves. It is as though there is an operative assumption that most of these events took place in caves. For example, Egeria mentions seven caves in her own surviving work, though Peter the Deacon lists nine caves when he relates her itinerary.[28] In several cases these caves are actually mentioned in Scripture, such as the "cleft" of Moses (Exod. 33:22), the cave of Elijah (I Kings 19:9), the cave of Abraham (Gen. 23:9), and the cave where Obadiah hid the prophets of the Lord (I Kings 18:4). Other caves are not explicitly mentioned in the Bible, but Egeria (and others) do not question the tradition associating caves with theophanies or other events, for example, the cave of Moses (Exod. 34) upon receiving the Law, the cave of

163

Elijah at Tishbe (I Kings 17:1), and the cave of the teaching of the Beatitudes of the Mount of Olives (Matt. 5:3-12). It is the events associated with the caves that interest Christians, not caves in and of themselves. It is simply that the embodiment of the tradition is associated with caves, for the most part. Since this appears to be already a developed tradition in Christian pilgrim texts, it may well have a Jewish antecedent.

John Wilkinson has pointed out that the third-century Christian baptismal creed and the *Te Deum Laudamus* ("We praise Thee, O God") of the sixth century implicitly express the connection with the land:[29]

The Baptismal Creed	Te Deum Laudamus
Dost thou believe in Christ Jesus the Son of God?	Thou art the King of Glory, O Christ.

1. **Bethlehem**

Who was born of Holy Spirit and the Virgin Mary,	Thou art the everlasting Son of the Father. When thou tookest upon thyself to deliver man; thou didst not abhor the Virgin's womb.

2. **Golgotha**

Who was crucified in the days of Pontius Pilate, And died, And rose the third day living from the dead,	When thou hadst overcome the sharpness of death: thou didst open the kingdom of heaven to all believers.

3. **Mount of Olives**

And ascended into the heaven, and sat down at the right hand of the Father, And will come to judge the living and the dead?	Thou sittest at the right hand of God in the glory of the Father. We believe that thou shalt come to be our judge.

Christian attachment to the land, then, moved from the explicit centrality of the land in the Gospels to an idealized Israel, such as one finds in I Peter 2:9 or Galatians 6:15-16. This concept is that of the nation, not of the land itself, though the biblical notion of the "people of God" was normally connected with the land. The next stage was recognition and reinforcement of the land itself and the events within Eretz Israel as normative for the growing institution of pilgrimage. The land as controlling theological concept was already implicit in the idea of pilgrimage. For Jews and Christians alike, then, cords of history and tradition bind them to the land.

9

Conclusions

This review of archaeological data pertinent to the study of the rabbis and the New Testament has been intended to introduce the student of Palestinian Judeo-Christian antiquity to the major issues within that field. It is not intended to be a systematic survey, for that is an impossibility, given the lack of methodological agreement in the study of Christian origins and Jewish history of the rabbinic period. Literary historians do not study and take into account the major findings of the archaeologist, and archaeologists are, in the main, not equipped to deal with the literary context of their discoveries. But we think it is now clear that both avenues of inquiry are necessary for a better understanding of the broad social and religious setting that influenced Roman Palestine. While many new scholarly studies are being produced from each side of the spectrum, very little significant synthetic work is being done on the social-historical interpretive aspects of these important disciplines.

Our modest aim, therefore, has been to bridge somewhat the large gap that has separated these independent areas within scholarship. When Goodenough undertook the monumental task of synthesizing the archaeological data available to him in the mid-1950s, it was his ardent hope that by the mid-1970s students of ancient Judaism and Christianity would be going beyond him. Unfortunately, this has not been the case and we might venture to say that his thirteen-volume work is used more by students of archaeology than by historians of religion. One reason for this sad state is the increasing specialization within the university in the 1960s and 1970s. When Goodenough taught at Yale, his courses were listed under religion, history, classics, psychology, and divinity. Today such an option is unthinkable. Also, the study of religion, which has only recently come into its own as an academic discipline, has not integrated the variety of data we have been talking about into its curriculum. The assumption is that tombs fall within the purview of anthropology; churches and synagogues within the purview of art history; and that epigraphy is studied in language departments.

We are not asking students of ancient Judaism or early Christianity to surrender any of their traditional interests. We are simply urging them to broaden their horizons and to recognize the fact that the present generation of scholars has already produced sufficient quantities of new data pertaining to such study to warrant serious review and attention. Students and teachers can no longer go their independent ways and hope to recreate faithfully the social setting of the world of the rabbis and the early Christian fathers. Moreover, just as there must be give-and-take between student and teacher, so too there must be a similar give-and-take among scholars.

In our review of the evidence from Galilee, we have noted how archaeology alone may help us understand better the modest literary sources at our disposal. Indeed, it is archaeological evidence that has already been sifted and interpreted that is so important to a renewed discussion of the setting of early Judaism. Galilee, the locus of classical Judaism as it emerges after the wars against Rome, also figures in the life of Jesus and in the emergence of the early church. It would seem gratuitous for us to underscore the importance of an adequate understanding of this region. A new, broadened approach to the study of Galilee enables us to understand many of the anomalies preserved in our literary sources. After an overview of the area, the variety there is understandable. That we may trace the bare outlines of both a conservatism and a Hellenism there greatly facilitates our ability to comprehend its dynamics. Galilee as revealed in archaeology and in literature emerges as a center of literary activity and material culture which is both tied to the past and open to the future.

Furthermore, it is archaeology and historical geography which have enabled us to describe the character of a rural center such as Nazareth, which at the same time was close to the busy trade routes of the day. If we relied solely on literary notices, we might conclude that nothing could be known of this village in the first century. The same might even be said of Capernaum, which, after all, does not figure largely in ancient Jewish sources outside the Gospels.

The surprise is Jerusalem. Here is a city that was the focus of attention of a whole nation for more than one thousand years prior to the first century C.E. Yet for all the descriptions of the center of national religious life, and by this we mean the Temple, we would surely miss the full cosmopolitan, urban character of this city if we relied on literary documentation alone.

Thus we are able to point out that the early Christian movement had to thread a new path as it advanced from rural agricultural centers such as Capernaum to the urban environment Jerusalem provided. It is therefore possible that the adherents of this predominantly rural movement had to overcome a certain urban snobbery in their early proclamations. Perhaps this is partially the explanation for the amazement of the "devout Jews" of Jerusalem gathered there at the Festival of Weeks (Pentecost) who said of the Twelve, "Are not all these who are speaking Galileans?" (Acts 2:7).

Our review of the problem of the languages of Palestine illustrates the use of archaeological data to gain new perspective. It is precisely the data that is so uninteresting to the historian that seems to shed so much light on the problem. We refer specifically to the graffiti on ossuaries and other scratchings in tombs. Students of the literary sources ordinarily view such data as beyond the purview of their discipline. Yet such informal epigraphy is so important precisely because of its lack of self-consciousness, its honesty, as it were. Such material is not produced for the public and therefore is relatively free of social and political bias.

Our discussion of Jewish tombs, burial practices, and views of afterlife has reinforced our methodological assumption that a study of the earliest Christian remains in Palestine means studying Jewish remains. Given the fact that Christianity did not develop its own symbolic vocabulary of signs and symbols until the fourth century, we must, so it seems, depend on Jewish remains in order to understand the context of early Christianity. The New Testament narrative presupposes a regular Jewish interment for Jesus, and an awareness of the archaeological realia of Jewish burial customs and tombs greatly illuminates our understanding of those passages that deal with the death of Jesus. On another level, a study of these realia provides an excellent opportunity for understanding anew the rabbinic texts which deal in a legal way with such matters.

When archaeological evidence is combined with a study of those texts which deal with beliefs in afterlife, especially since there is much epigraphic data from tombs, a unique opportunity is presented. In such an instance, both the dominant Semitic perceptions of man as a solitary unity and the later Hellenistic view of man as a divided entity may be followed in some detail. An awareness of the great fluidity of ideas about afterlife in Roman Palestine can provide vivid witness to the lengthy process of acculturation and accommodation which preceded the Late Roman period. Should a methodological consensus arise regarding either the presence of Jewish Christianity or its precise whereabouts in this

169

period, it would not be at all difficult to examine its purported archaeological traces as they pertain to such matters as well.

The issue of early Christian evidences still remains one of the major unresolved questions in the archaeology of the Holy Land. It is the period between Bar Kokhba (135 c.e.) and Constantine (330 c.e.), or roughly two centuries, which remains the dark ages in our survey. It is our fervent hope that the discussion here if nothing else will at least further the possibility of renewed interest in this period.

With regard to the churches and synagogues of Palestine, several important historical inferences are to be drawn. First, it is not an easy matter to rely on either churches or synagogues in the reconstruction of the religious setting of the first centuries of the common era. The fact that most of the material evidence is late suggests a great deal about the nature of early Jewish and Christian communities in Palestine. While Herod the Great was organizing one of the greatest building campaigns of antiquity, the seeds of classical Judaism were being sown in the meeting places of the likes of Hillel the Elder. When Rome was tightening its yoke upon the administration of Judaea, a community of Jesus' followers was articulating a view of the future that required little of this world in the way of material culture. It is therefore not surprising that while we have many material remains of a monumental nature, the physical evidences of the early Christian community and of early Pharisaism are meager indeed. Because the first Christian century is so diverse in cultural matters and so pluralistic in social and religious elements, it is important for us to relate the present data to the appropriate social setting. It is a matter of not a little irony that we are forced to view this formative period through the eyes of one so detested as Herod and his followers. But we have also underscored how important it is to realize the urban and cosmopolitan pressures of this era as well.

Second, a study of the churches and synagogues of ancient Palestine reveals a variety that bespeaks of the multidimensional aspects of the communities of faith which produced them. Architectural eclecticism is but one facet of this development. In view of the increasing importance of holy men and holy places in both traditions, a growing sense of the centrality of the land is to be discerned, along with a greater appreciation for the deeds of venerated men and women of the sacred community. In Judaism this tendency is reflected in monumental funerary art and architecture and the custom of reburial, all of which seem to find a place in the Christian tradition. By the medieval period, even a synagogue (e.g., Meiron) is built on the purported burial site of holy men, Hillel and Bar Yochai. This phenomenon is not unlike the cult of martyrs and reliquaries in Christian churches, where often a holy man or martyr was buried in a commemorative spot such as we found in a church at Pella.

In both traditions the end result of this is the notion of pilgrimage, or going up to the land and its sacred sites. To this very day, Jews and Christians perform this sacred act, as do the Muslims, striving as it were to experience anew the spirit of long ago and to collapse the boundaries of time between now and then, a feat somehow facilitated in the places where sacred deeds were done.

On a more general level we may remark that our multidimensional approach to the study of early Palestinian Judaism and early Christianity has left us with an impression of cultural diversity in this formative era. While assessing the degree of accommodation to Hellenism is often a very complex matter, the languages used in Palestine and the regions of their attested usage reflect the diverse crosscurrents affecting the rabbis and church fathers. Where one chose to live was apparently a conscious decision influenced as much by social and economic concerns as by religious preferences. The choice between urban life over against rural or surburban life might well have provided the stuff of a family dilemma in antiquity as it does today. While many individual families aspired to and achieved great wealth (for example, the Bar

Kathros family of first-century Jerusalem or the family of the Patrician House in fourth-century Meiron), simpler, more modest families of less means coexisted side by side with them. We need not necessarily assume that the wealthier families were the more assimilated; rather, it is the total context of the evidence they leave behind which should determine our assessment of their values.

For all the indications of cultural diversity in late antiquity, there is a recognizable homogeneity of culture as well. It is as important to stress the forces of continuity which bind the past inextricably to the present as it is to point to the emergent forces of discontinuity which enable change to occur. It is clear to us that a genuine sense of conservatism in burial customs lingers on into late antiquity and greatly affects views of afterlife and even influences the modest nature of grave goods which are left behind. Conservatism in art goes hand in hand with a kind of self-conscious attempt to preserve Hebrew/ Aramaic culture and characterizes the extreme north of ancient Palestine. It is such a force of continuity which enables us to measure the extent to which new forces have come to dominate.

Palestinian Judaism of the early centuries of the common era is not unlike Palestinian Judaism in the time of Jesus if we collect many diverse phenomena under a single rubric. The inferences we have drawn are on the basis of evidences not usually assessed, and though such a conclusion may seem to reflect what has come to be a post-Qumran consensus, the details of diversity fall into categories usually not considered in standard treatments of the subject. Judaism of the first century is surely more than a grouping of religious sects, and surely earliest Christianity cannot be monolithic either.

Our presentation has also shown how tenuous the relationship between material culture and the reality behind it may be. The Herodian Temple of Jerusalem may rank as one of the great cult centers of the Eastern Mediterranean world, but it surely reflects only limited aspects of the religion and culture of the first century of our era. Usually the reverse of this situation obtains, that is, the level of material culture will be relatively low in comparison with a high level of creativity documented in other spheres such as religion and literature. Still, the study of literature alone, produced and edited by an intellectual elite, can only present us with exaggerations and distortions and little regard for popular religion and culture. Artifactual data that is random and not self-conscious can provide the historian with a helpful corrective.

It is with the hope that this work will contribute to further refinement in our understanding of the dual heritage spawned long ago in Palestine that we offer the present study as a prolegomenon, or invitation, to future work.

Journal Abbreviations

AASOR	*Annual of the American Schools of Oriental Research*
BA	*Biblical Archeologist*
BAR	*Biblical Archaeological Review*
BASOR	*Bulletin of the American Schools of Oriental Research*
EI	*Eretz Israel*
HTR	*Harvard Theological Review*
IEJ	*Israel Exploration Journal*
JBL	*Journal of Biblical Literature*
JQR	*Jewish Quarterly Review*
LA	*Liber Annuus*
PEQ	*Palestinian Exploration Quarterly*
RB	*Revue Biblique*
SH	*Studia Hierosolymitana*
ZDPV	*Zeitschrift des deutschen Palästina-Vereins*

Notes

1. Introduction: The Relevance of Nonliterary Sources

1. Bargil Pixner, "An Essene Quarter on Mount Zion?" in *Studia Hierosolymitana* (1976), 245-84.

2. We accept the historical geography of the Balata-Sychem area as evidence for the setting of John 4. We are saying that we have no direct evidence for St. John the apostle or any of the others, except perhaps St. Peter. This is why we use indirect evidence such as archaeology to reconstruct the probable type of Judaism practiced by Jesus, et al.

2. The Cultural Setting of Galilee

1. For a convenient resumé see Yochanan Aharoni, "Survey in Galilee: Israelite Settlements and Their Pottery," *EI*, 4 (1956), 56-64 (Heb.); for a full presentation see his *"The Settlement of the Israelite Tribes in Upper Galilee"* (Ph.D. diss., Hebrew University, 1955 [Heb]).

2. The authors' most recent statement on this subject appears as E. M. Meyers, J. F. Strange, and Dennis E. Groh, "The Meiron Excavation Project: Archaeological Survey in Galilee and Golan," 1976, 230 (1978), 1-24. For a popular and convenient summary of these views see the small volume *Galilee and Regionalism,* in *Explor* 3 (winter 1977).

3. The notable publications of this group include Bellarmino Bagatti, *Antichi Villaggi Christiani di Galilea,* publication of the Stadium Biblicum Franciscanum, Collectio Minor, no. 13 (Jerusalem: Franciscan Press, 1971) and his *The Church from the Gentiles in Palestine, ibid.,* no. 4 (1971); Ignazio Mancini, *Archaeological Discoveries Relative to the Judaeo-Christians, ibid.,* no. 10 (1970); and the four-volume report on the Capernaum excavations, especially Emmanuele Testa's *I graffiti della casa di S. Pietro, ibid.,* no. 19 (1972).

3a. See, e.g., Acts 8:5-25, 40; 9:10, 31; 9:32–10:48, *passim.*

3b. See Reuven Kimelman, "Rabbi Yochanan and Jewish Christianity: New Evidence for Identification of Third Century *Minim* with Gnosticizing Jewish Christians," in E. P. Sanders and A. Baumgarten, eds., *Normative Self-Definition in Judaism from the Maccabees to Mid-Third Century* [The McMaster's Project: Symposium II], forthcoming (Philadelphia: Fortress Press).

4. Samuel Safrai and Menahem Stern, eds., *The Jewish People in the First Century*, 2 vols. (Philadelphia: Fortress Press, 1974, 1976); the new edition of Emil Schuerer's *The History of the Jewish People in the Age of Jesus Christ (175 B.C.E.–C.E. 135)*, rev. and ed. Geza Vermes and Fergus Millar (Edinburgh: T. & T. Clark, 1973); and *The World History of the Jewish People: The Herodian Period*, ed. Michael Avi-Yonah (Jerusalem: Masada Press, 1975).

5. For a review of recent literature see the essay of E. M. Meyers, "Recent Literature of the Archaeology of Eretz Israel," *Jewish Book Annual*, 36 (New York: Jewish Book Council, 1978), pp. 88-96.

6. Some of this material is published in Meyers, Strange, and Groh, "The Meiron Excavation Project," figs. 1–8. See also the article on ceramic material published by E. M. Meyers, A. T. Kraabel, and J. F. Strange in *Ancient Synagogue Excavations at Khirbet Shema'* (Durham: Duke University Press, 1976) and *AASOR*, no. 42, pp. 9-21.

7. See below on Jerusalem, chapter 3 pp. 49-56.

8. Well-known proponents of such a view would include R. H. Lightfoot, *Locality and Doctrine in the Gospels* (New York: Harper, 1937), pp. 125, 143; Ernst Lohmeyer, *Galilaea und Jerusalem* (Göttingen: Vandenhoeck & Ruprecht, 1936); and Willi Marxsen, *Mark the Evangelist: Studies on the Redaction History of the Gospel* (Nashville: Abingdon, 1969), pp. 83-92. In addition to the view that Galilee had special theological significance in the messianic scheme of things, several scholars have argued for a much broader definition of Galilee that would include Upper Galilee and the Golan Heights up to Damascus. See Naphtali Wieder, *The Judean Scrolls and Karaism* (London: East and West Library, 1962), pp. 22-23. Additional references to the theological significance of Galilee in its broader meaning are collected by Guenter Stemberger, "Galilee: Land of Salvation," in W. D. Davies, *The Gospel and the Land: Early Christianity and Jewish Territorial Doctrine* (Berkeley: University of California Press, 1974). The fact that the authors argue for a strong cultural continuity in Upper Galilee–Golan in the first centuries tends to support the idea that the Jerusalem-Judaean exiles conceived of the entire northern area as a refuge after the two Roman wars. The reticence of the early rabbis toward the special theological doctrines associated with Galilee may be due to the fact that such views were largely associated with the early Christians. By the medieval period, however, the rabbis are clearly enunciating a strong doctrine of a messianic precursor in Galilee. On this latter point see Wieder, *Judean Scrolls*, pp. 50-51.

9. Geza Vermes, *Jesus the Jew: A Historian's Reading of the Gospels* (London: Collins, 1973).

10. John G. Gager, *Kingdom and Community: The Social World of Early Christianity* (Englewood Cliffs, N.J.: Prentice-Hall, 1975), pp. 26-27.

11. Davies, *The Gospel and the Land*, pp. 366 ff.

12. Geza Vermes's dependency on limited textual evidence may be found in *Jesus the Jew*, pp. 52ff., 237-43. Cf. also Jacob Neusner, *A Life of Rabbi Yohanan ben Zakkai* (Leiden: E. J. Brill, 1962), pp. 27-32, and Salo W. Baron, *A Social and Religious History of the Jews* (New York: Columbia University Press, 1952), vol. I, pp. 276-80, 414-15. For a popularly held Christian scholarly view see L. E. Elliott-Binns, *Galilean Christianity*, Studies in Biblical Theology, no. 16 (London: SCM Press, 1956), p. 17.

13. Aharon Oppenheimer, *The 'Am Ha-aretz: A Study in the Social History of the Jewish People in the Hellenistic-Roman Period* (Leiden: E. J. Brill, 1977).

14. *Ibid.*, pp. 200-217.

15. Such a view has been previously advanced by E. M. Meyers in "Galilean Regionalism as a Factor in Historical Reconstruction," *BASOR*, 220:221 (1975-76); pp. 93-101.

16. Such is the contention of F. X. Malinowski, *Galilean Judaism in the Writings of Flavius Josephus* (Ph.D. diss., Duke University, 1973).

17. *Antiquities* 5.63 5.86; 5.92. Cf. the earlier apocryphal works of Tobit 1:2 and Judith 1:7-8, which also mention Upper Galilee and assume such a twofold division. Strangely enough, neither the Hebrew Bible nor the New Testament mentions such a division, which is doubtless a reflection of the administrative system imposed in all Galilee in the Hellenistic and Roman periods. For further elaboration on the border situation in Galilee, see Samuel Klein, *Eretz ha-Galil* (Jerusalem: Mosad ha-Rav Cock, 1945), pp. 139-46 (Heb.), and Michael Avi-Yonah, *The Holy Land from the Persian to the Arab Conquest (536 B.C.E.-C.E. 640)* (Grand Rapids: Baker, 1966), pp. 106, 135-42 (Lower Galilee), and pp. 97, 112, 133-35 (Upper Galilee).

18. *Antiquities* 8.142; *Wars* 3.35-39.

19. Herbert Danby, ed. and trans. *The Mishnah* (Oxford: Clarendon Press, 1933), *Sev.* 9.2.

20. Josephus does, however, use the phrase "all Galilee" in a variety of contexts connoting both urban and rural areas of the north and south; *Antiquities* 14.395; 14.415; *Life* 28; 132; 206; *Wars* 2.589.

21. Danby, *Sev.* 9.2.

22. Avi-Yonah, *The Holy Land*, pp. 133-35; Klein, *Eretz ha-Galil*, p. 129, especially for discussion of the identification of Kefar Inan. For an excellent presentation of the geological/geographical situation in Galilee see Yehuda Karmon, *Israel: A Regional Geography* (London: John Wiley—Interscience, 1971), pp. 161-212.

23. Denis Baly, *The Geography of the Bible* (London: Lutterworth Press, 1958), p. 189.

24. See Yochanan Aharoni, *The Land of the Bible: A Historical Geography* (London: Burns & Oates, 1967), p. 25.

25. Avi-Yonah, *The Holy Land*, p. 134, map 11.

26. *Ibid.*, pp. 167, 170. Technically the east side of Upper Galilee was Ulatha in the ancient world. Our contention is that it is administratively part of Upper Galilee.

27. *Antiquities* 17.283; *Life* 213-14; *Wars* 2.188; 3.35; 3.38.

28. The attention devoted to Gischala is doubtless a reflection of Josephus' intense rivalry with John son of Levi. David Rhoads, in *Israel in Revolution, 6–74 c.e.* (Philadelphia: Fortress Press, 1976), p. 133, maintains that the revolution of John in Galilee was not directed against Rome but against Josephus himself.

29. *Wars* 2.573.

30. See S. B. F. Brandon, *Jesus and the Zealots: A Study of the Political Factor in Primitive Christianity* (Manchester University Press, 1967), *passim*, for the most extreme statement on this matter. John Gager, *Kingdom and Community*, also evaluates the zealot movement from a social-anthropological point of view. Other key treatments of the problem include Martin Hengel, *Die Zeloten* (Leiden: E. J. Brill, 1961); Morton Smith, "Zealots and Sicarii: Their Origins and Relation," *Harvard Theological Review, 64 (1971);* William R. Farmer, *Maccabees, Zealots, and Josephus* (New York: Columbia University Press, 1956). See Rhoads, *Israel in Revolution, passim.*

31. *Wars* 5.142.

32. *Life* 104-5.

33. *Wars* 2.585-90. The extent of John of Gischala's activities in Galilee is very difficult to recover. Judging from his challenge to Josephus' command there, he made substantial inroads and was successful in summoning many people in the area to join in the Jerusalem war against Rome.

34. *Antiquities* 17.288-89; *Wars* 2.68.

35. *Wars* 2.503.

36. Rhoads, *Israel in Revolution*, p. 176.

37. While the conclusions reached by the authors about this area stretching from Upper Galilee–West Golan are based on personal site visits and surveys conducted over the past five years (see esp. Meyers, Strange, and Groh, "The Meiron Excavation Project"), they happily acknowledge the assistance of Dan Urman, Secretary, Archaeological Survey of Israel, for his close and willing cooperation. In particular, his list of Golan sites, which was prepared to tie in with the Israel Department of Antiquities' *List of Monuments,* has been of enormous help to the authors.

38. Avi-Yonah, *The Holy Land*, p. 191.

39. Baly, *Geography of the Bible*, pp. 189-91.

40. Avi-Yonah, *The Holy Land*, p. 112.

41. By administrative capital we are to understand the place that possesses "the royal bank and offices"; so A. H. Jones, "The Urbanization of Palestine," *Journal of Roman Studies,* 21 (1931), 81. By the fourth century "the whole of the Judaeo-Samaritan territory, excluding the Jordan Valley, has been . . . absorbed into a series of pagan city-states. . . . Their desire to shine as promoters of Hellenistic civilization seems, however, to have been tempered on the one hand by a lingering fear of offending the religious susceptibilities of their subjects, and on the other by a reluctance to lose control of revenue-producing territory." *Ibid.,* 84. Cf. A. H. Jones's remarks on this problem in *The Cities of the Eastern Roman Provinces,* 2d ed. (Oxford: Clarendon Press, 1971), pp. 274 ff. and notes. Jones's manuscript was revised by Avi-Yonah. We take Josephus' term *tetracomia* for the administration of Upper Galilee quite literally, to wit, in the sense of four villages scattered

over the area. The very designation, therefore, incicates a highly decentralized administrative setup which contrasts sharply with other areas. The situation in the Golan was very similar. Included in Provincia Judaea after Agrippa II, the last of the Herodian dynasty, like Upper Galilee, the Golan remained outside the city areas. See Avi-Yonah, *The Holy Land,* pp. 110-12 and Jones, "The Urbanization of Palestine," p. 84.

42. Baly, *Geography of the Bible,* p. 189.

43. In the time of Hadrian, Sepphoris was renamed Diocaesarea, but it had been granted full municipal rights in the time of Vespasian. See Avi-Yonah, *The Holy Land,* p. 111, n. 13.

44. See Oppenheimer, *The 'Am Ha-aretz.* While this is not the place to argue the reliability of the literary witnesses to Galilean Judaism in the first centuries c.e., reference should also be made to Adolph Buechler's other classic statement, *Der Galilaeische 'Am-ha 'Ares des zweiten Jahrhunderts* (Vienna: A. Hoelder, 1906; reprinted Hildesheim, Georg Olms Verlagsbuchhandlung, 1968). We have already referred to the thesis of Malinowski, who contends that Judaism in Galilee as portrayed by Josephus indicates that the Galilean, like other Jews, practiced the Law and interpreted it, pp. 187-88. He finds at least some support for his views in the work of Selah Merrill, *Galilee in the Time of Christ* (Boston: Congregational Publishing Society, 1881), p. 86. Malinowski conjectures that Yohanan ben Zakkai's lament on Galilee resulted from the fact that he was consulted so seldom. Against the view of the reliability of Josephus as a witness for Galilean Pharisaic Judaism, see Morton Smith, "Palestinian Judaism in the First Century," in *Israel: Its Role in Civilization,* ed. Moshe Davis (New York: Seminary Institute of the Jewish Theological Seminary of America, Harper, 1956), pp. 67-81 and Jacob Neusner, "Josephus's Pharisees," in *Ex Orbe Religionum Studia Geo Widengren Oblata,* vol. I (Leiden: E. J. Brill, 1972), 224-44. Josephus, to be sure, had reasons for presenting the Pharisaic movement in a positive light after the war with Rome, but it remains to be seen whether or not his statements on Galilean Judaism can be deemed trustworthy. Vermes' other major statement on Galilean Judaism may be found in "Hanina ben Dosa," *Journal of Jewish Studies,* 23 (1972), 28-50, which conforms with the general picture he presents in *Jesus the Jew.*

45. The artistic remains at Beth She 'arim, are evaluated by many, but see M. Avi-Yonah, "The Leda Coffin from Beth She 'arim, *EI,* 8 (1967), 143-48 (Heb.). For a general statement of this problem see his *Oriental Art in Roman Palestine* (Rome: Centro di Studi Semitica, Instituto di Studi del vicino oriente, Universita, 1961). For a complete consideration of Beth She 'arim see the three volumes now available in Hebrew and English and our discussion in chapters 5 and 7.

46. Avi-Yonah, *The Holy Land,* p. 11.

47. *Ibid.,* p. 112.

47a. This material has been conveniently published for the Meiron Excavation Project as No. 2 in its series by Richard S. Hanson, *Tyrian Influence in the Upper Galilee.* (Cambridge: ASOR, 1980).

48. *Ibid.,* p. 113. This datum also casts great doubt on the "zealot theory."

49. See Samuel Klein's '*Ever ha-Yarden*, republished in *Selected Articles on the Golan* (by the Qibbutz Movement), pp. 78-161, n.d. (Heb.).

50. The Middle to Late Roman period is discussed by Saul Lieberman, "Palestine in the Third and Fourth Centuries," *Jewish Quarterly Review*, 37 (1947), 31-54. Study of the Meiron materials has shown that the site was abandoned in the time of Constantine II, when apparently the tax burden had become so great that it forced the population to disperse. Lieberman rejects the possibility that the revolt of Gallus could have had any repercussions so far inland as Meiron; the authors are inclined to agree. E. M. Meyers, C. L. Meyers, and J. F. Strange, "Excavations at Ancient Meiron in Upper Galilee, 1974–1975, Second Preliminary Report," *AASOR*, 43 (1978), 73-108, confirms these contentions of Lieberman.

51. Half-brother of Julian, Gallus reigned in Antioch from 351 to 354 c.e. In addition to putting down a revolt in Palestine, he quelled rebellion in Issauria as well. He was recalled by Constantine II and executed in 354. His reign is regarded as oppressive and bloody.

3. The Context of Early Christianity and Palestinian Judaism

1. Although Jerusalem was an important center for certain governmental functions, Caesarea was the capital.

2. Yigal Shiloh, "Tables of Major Archaeological Activities in Jerusalem since 1863," in *Jerusalem Revealed*, ed. Yigael Yadin, (Jerusalem: Israel Exploration Society, 1975), pp. 131-35; also published in Michael Avi-Yonah, ed., *Encyclopedia of Archaeological Excavations in the Holy Land*, vol. II (Englewood Cliffs, N.J.: Prentice-Hall, 1975), pp. 643-47.

3. Charles Wilson and Charles Warren, *The Recovery of Jerusalem* (London: R. Bentley, 1871); Charles Warren, *Underground Jerusalem*, ed. W. Morrison (London: R. Bentley, 1871).

4. Wilson and Warren, *Recovery of Jerusalem*.

5. Shiloh, "Tables of Major Archaeological Activities in Jerusalem"; Raymond Weill, *La Cité de David*, 2 vols. (Paris: P. Geuthner, 1920, 1947).

6. Weill, *Cité de David*.

7. Benjamin Mazar, "The Excavations in the Old City of Jerusalem, Preliminary Report of the First Season, 1968," *EI*, 9 (1969), 1-21; Michael Avi-Yonah, "The Latin Inscription from the Excavations in Jerusalem," *ibid.*, 22-24; Mazar, "The Excavations in the Old City of Jerusalem near the Temple Mount, Preliminary Report of the Second and Third Seasons, 1969–1970," *ibid.*, 10 (1971), 1-36; *idem, The Mountain of the Lord* (Garden City, N.Y.: Doubleday, 1975); *idem*, "The Archaeological Excavations near the Temple Mount," *Jerusalem Revealed*, pp. 25-40.

8. Nahman Avigad, "Excavations in the Jewish Quarter of the Old City, 1969–1971," in *Jerusalem Revealed*, pp. 41-51; *idem*, "Excavations in the Jewish Quarter of the Old City, Jerusalem, 1969–1970 (Preliminary Report)," *IEJ*, 20 (1970), 1-8; *idem*, "Excavations in the Jewish Quarter of the Old City, Jerusalem, 1970 (Preliminary Report II)," ibid., 129-40; *idem*, "Excavations in the Jewish Quarter of the Old City of Jerusalem, 1971 (Third Preliminary Report)," *ibid.*, 22 (1972), 193-200.

9. F. J. Bliss and A. C. Dickie, *Excavations at Jerusalem 1894–1897*, (London: Committee of the Palestine Exploration Fund, 1898).

10. Magen Broshi, "Excavations in the House of Caiaphas, Mt. Zion," in *Jerusalem Revealed*, pp. 57-60.

11. C. N. Johns, "The Citadel, Jerusalem," *Quarterly of the Department of Antiquities of Palestine*, 14 (1950), 121-90.

12. M. Avi-Yonah, "Jerusalem of the Second Temple Period," *Jerusalem Revealed*, pp. 9-13 For a demurrer see John Wilkinson, *Jerusalem as Jesus Knew It: Archaeology as Evidence* (London: Thames and Hudson, 1978), pp. 56-65; also Kathleen Kenyon, *Digging Up Jerusalem* (London: n.p , 1974); John Wilkinson, "The Streets of Jerusalem," *Levant*, 7 (1975), 18-36.

13. On "Herod the Elder" see "Herod," *Encyclopedia Judaica*. "Herod the Elder" is a modern pejorative term. During his life he was called ' Herod' or "Herod of Judaea" or "King Herod." After his death he was called "Herod the Great" to distinguish him from his sons who were Ethnarchs and Tetrarchs and his grandsons who bore the title of "King."

14. Ruth Amiran, "Herod's Palace," *IEJ*, 22 (1972), 51-52. R. Amiran and A. Eitan, "Excavations in the Jerusalem Citadel," *Jerusalem Revealed*, pp. 52-54.

15. Wilkinson, see note 12 above and Strange's forthcoming review of Wilkinson in *BASOR*.

16. M. I. Rostovtsev *et al.*, eds., *The Excavations at Dura-Europos* (New Haven: Yale University Press, 1943; London: Oxford University Press, 1943).

17. Magen Broshi, "Estimating the Population of Ancient Jerusalem," *Biblical Archaeology Review*, 4 (1978), 10-15; John Wilkinson, "Ancient Jerusalem, Its Water Supply and Population," *PEQ*, 106 (1978), 33-51 Magen Broshi, "La population de l'ancienne Jerusalem," *RB*, 82 (1975), 5-14.

18. Jack Finegan, *Archaeology of the New Testament* (Princeton University Press, 1969), p. 115.

19. This is based on a calculation of one square meter per person, for a rather close grouping but not a dense crowd.

20. Finegan, *Archaeology of the New Testament*, p. 118.

21. Mazar, *Mountain of the Lord*, p. 112.

22. Finegan, *Archaeology of the New Testament*, pp. 119-20, and the bibliography cited there; see also chapter 4, pp. 82-83.

23. Mazar, *Mountain of the Lord*, pp. 126-30.

24. Avigad, "The Architecture of Jerusalem in the Second Temple Period," *Jerusalem Revealed*, pp. 14-20.

25. See the photos in *Jerusalem Revealed*, pp. 28-29, or in Mazar, *Mountain of the Lord*, p. 124

26. *Jerusalem Revealed*, p. 27, (illustration on p. 35).

27. *Ibid.*, pp. 27-28.

28. Mazar, *The Mountain of the Lord*, pp. 126-27. Most scholars believe the present form of the triple gate is medieval.

29. *Jerusalem Revealed*, pp. 31-32. See J. Fitzmyer, "The Aramaic qorban Inscription from Jebel Hallet et Turi and Mark 7:1/Matthew 15:5," *JBL*, 78 (1959), 60-65.

183

30. Avigad, "Excavations in the Jewish Quarter 1969–1971," pp. 46-47.

31. *Ibid.*, p. 47.

32. Pierre Benoit, "The Archaeological Reconstruction of the Antonia Fortress," in *Jerusalem Revealed*, pp. 7-90.

33. On Bethesda see Antoine Duprez, *Jésus et les dieux Guérisseurs, à propos de Jean V* (Paris: Gabalda, 1970); Joachim Jeremias, *The Rediscovery of Bethesda, John 5:2* (Louisville: Southern Baptist Theological Seminary, 1966).

34. For a convenient summary of the archaeological and literary notices on Nazareth see Finegan, *Archaeology of the New Testament*, pp. 27-32. See also Bellarmino Bagatti, *Excavations in Nazareth*, vol. 1, publication of the Studium Biblicum Franciscanum, no. 17 (Jerusalem: Franciscan Press, 1969).

35. Bagatti, *Excavations in Nazareth*, vol. 1. Note the silos and cisterns in foldout plate XI.

36. *Ibid.* Middle Bronze to Late Bronze pottery, comprising the contents of three tombs, appears on pp. 258-68. Pottery of the Iron II period is from two silos, see pp. 269-72. Pottery of the late Hellenistic to Byzantine and later periods is spread about the site, see pp. 272-318.

37. Samuel Klein, *Beiträge zur Geographie und Geschichte Galiläas* (Leipzig: Hinrichs, 1909).

38. Finegan, *Archaeology of the New Testament*, p. 29 and bibliography.

39. J. F. Strange, "Capernaum," *Interpreter's Dictionary of the Bible, Supplementary Volume* (Nashville: Abingdon, 1976), pp. 140-41.

40. Stanislao Loffreda, *A Visit to Capharnaum* (Jerusalem: Franciscan Press, 1972), p. 20; see also Strange, "Capernaum," p. 140; and Wilson and Warren, *Recovery of Jerusalem*, p. 269.

41. Thus correcting the data presented in Loffreda, *A Visit to Capharnaum*, and Strange, "Capernaum." But see Virgilio Corbo, "Aspetti Urbanistici de Cafarnao," *Liber Annuus*, 21 (1971), 263-85.

42. Michael Avi-Yonah, *The Holy Land* (Grand Rapids: Baker, 1966), p. 138.

43. Virgilio Corbo, "Nuovi Scavi Archaeologici nella Sinagoga de Cafarnao," 20 (1970), 7-52; Corbo, "La Sinagoga de Cafarnao dopo gli Scavi del 1972," *ibid.*, 22 (1972), 204-35; Loffreda, "The Synagogue of Capharnaum: Archaeological Evidence for Its Late Chronology," *ibid.*, 5-29; Corbo, "Sotto la Sinagoga de Cafarnao un'insula della citta," *ibid.*, 27 (1977), 156-72; Corbo, "Edifici antichi sotto la sinagoga de Cafarnao," vol. 1 (Jerusalem: Franciscan Press, 1976), pp. 159-76.

44. J. F. Strange, "Magdala," *Interpreter's Dictionary of the Bible, Supplementary Volume*, p. 561 and bibliography there.

45. Loffreda, *A Visit to Capharnaum*, 6th ed. (Jerusalem: Franciscan Press, 1978), pp. 23-24.

46. Virgilio Corbo, *The House of Saint Peter at Capharnaum: A Preliminary Report of the First Two Campaigns of Excavations*, publication of the Stadium Biblicum Franciscanum, Collectio Minor, no. 5 (Jerusalem: Franciscan Press, 1969). See also note 40 above.

47. Asher Ovadiah, *Corpus of the Byzantine Churches in the Holy Land* (Bonn: Peter Hanstein, 1970), especially those at Jerusalem (the Ascension

and the Tomb of the Virgin), Mount Gerizim (the Woman at the Well of Sychar, John 4), Bethlehem (the Constantinian church), and see pp. 214-15.

48. For the pottery see Stanislao Loffreda, *Cafarnao II: La Ceramica,* publication of the Studium Biblicum Franciscanum, no. 19 (Jerusalem: Franciscan Press, 1974).

49. Emmanuele Testa, *Cafarnao IV: I Graffiti della casa de San Pietro,* publication of the Studium Biblicum Franciscanum, no. 19 (Jerusalem: Franciscan Press, 1972).

50. John Wilkinson, *Egeria's Travels* (London: SPCK, 1971), p. 194: "Moreover, in Capernaum the house of the *prince of the apostles* has been made into a church, with its original walls still standing."

51. Loffreda, *A Visit to Capharnaum,* p. 23.

4. The Languages of Roman Palestine

1. The oldest known Hebrew writing to date is the ostracon from 'Izbet Sartah in Israel, reported in BA, 39 (1976), 87; for Aramaic see E. Y. Kutscher, "Aramaic," *Encyclopedia Judaica,* vol. 3, cols. 259-60.

2. Jacob M. Meyers. The Anchor Bible, *Ezra, Nehemiah,* vol. 14 (Garden City, N.Y.: Doubleday, 1965), p. 150, comment, p. 151.

3. The most recent introduction to the scrolls and their relation to early Judaism and emerging Christianity is that of Geza Vermes, *The Dead Sea Scrolls: Qumran in Perspective* (London: Collins, 1977).

4. There is no convenient corpus of ossuary inscriptions. A brief discussion appears in Jack Finegan, *The Archaeology of the New Testament* (Princeton University Press, 1969), pp. 216-19. The recent doctoral dissertations at the Hebrew University in Jerusalem of Pablo Figueras and L. Y. Rahmani are helpful in highlighting additional unpublished materials. (For details see Y. Barnai, ed., *Yad Izhak ben-Zvi,* which lists Ph.D. dissertations in Israeli Universities.)

5. The ossuaries from Dominus Flevit on the Mount of Olives form the core of these data; however, they have not been published in English. The student is referred to Bellarmino Bagatti and J. T. Milik, *Gli Scavi del 'Dominus Flevit,"* part 1: *Le Necropoli del Periodo Romano,* publication of the Studium Biblicum Fraciscanum, no. 13 (Jerusalem: Franciscan Press, 1958).

6. For previous studies in this general area of the languages of Palestine in the first century, see the following: Saul Lieberman. *Greek in Jewish Palestine* (New York: Jewish Theological Seminary of America, 1942) and *Hellenism in Jewish Palestine* (*ibid.,* 1950), which includes corrections and additions to the earlier volume; Martin Hengel, *Judaism and Hellenism,* trans. John Bowden, 2 vols. (Philadelphia: Fortress Press, 1974); Joseph Fitzmyer, "The Languages of Palestine in the First Century A.D.," *Catholic Biblical Quarterly,* 32 (1970), 501-31; John C. James, *The Language of Palestine and Adjacent Regions* (Edinburgh: T. & T. Clark, 1920); Harris Birkeland, *The Language of Jesus* (Oslo: Dybwad, 1954); Birger Gerhardsson, *Memory and Manuscript* (Lund: Gleerup/Copenhagen: Munksgaard, 1961); James Barr. "Which Language Did Jesus Speak? Some Remarks of a Semiticist," *Bulletin of the John Rylands Library,* 53:1 (1970), 9-29; J. A. Emerton, "The Problem of

Vernacular Hebrew in the First Century A.D. and the Language of Jesus," *Journal of Theological Studies*, 24:1 (1973), 1-23; A. W. Argyle, "Greek among the Jews of Palestine in New Testament Times," *New Testament Studies*, 20:1 (1973), 87-89; P. Lapide, "Insights from Qumran into the Languages of Jesus," *Revue de Qumran*, 8:4 (1975), 483-501; Kurt Treu, "Die Bedeutung des Griechischen für die Juden im Römischen Reich," *Kairos: Zeitschrift für Religionswissenschaft und Theologie*, 15 (1973), 123-44.

7. See note 1, above.

8. See Joseph Ziegler, ed., *Sapientia Iesu Filii Sirach* (Göttingen: Vandenhoeck & Ruprecht, 1965), p. 127 (Greek text).

9. Yigael Yadin, *The Ben Sira Scroll from Masada* (Jerusalem: Israel Exploration Society, 1965).

10. J. T. Milik, *Ten Years of Discovery in the Wilderness of Judaea*, Studies in Biblical Theology, no. 26 (London: SCM, 1959), p. 130. Milik is of the opinion that "Mishnaic Hebrew was the normal language of the Judaean population in the Roman period."

11. The standard edition of the Copper Scroll is in Maurice Baillet, J. T. Milik, and Roland de Vaux, *Discoveries in the Judaean Desert of Jordan*, vol. 3: *Les petites grottes de Qumran* (Oxford: Clarendon Press, 1962), pp. 211-302.

12. See Jean-Baptiste Frey, *Corpus Inscriptionem Judaicarum*, vol. 2 (Vaticano: Pont. Ist. di Arch. Crist., 1952), for a convenient summary.

13. A short account of these lids is in Bellarmino Bagatti, *The Church from the Circumcision: History and Archaeology of the Judaeo-Christians*, publication of the Studium Biblicum Franciscanum, Collectio Minor, no. 2 (Jerusalem: Franciscan Press, 1971), p. 277.

14. See note 5 above.

15. Nahman Avigad, "The Tomb of the Nazirite on Mount Scopus," in *Jerusalem Revealed* (Jerusalem: Israel Exploration Society, 1975), pp. 66-67.

16. The text is in Finegan, *Archaeology of the New Testament*, pp. 192-93.

17. Benjamin Mazar, "The Archaeological Excavations near the Temple Mount," *Jerusalem Revealed*, pp. 31-32, p. 35.

18. *Ibid.*, pp. 26-27, photo p. 35.

19. Many of the Masada finds are published in the popular work of Yadin, *Ben Sira Scroll from Masada*. For a more detailed discussion, see Yadin, *Masada: First Season of Excavations 1963–1964, Preliminary Report*, III (Jerusalem: Israel Exploration Society, 1965), especially the chapter "Documents and Inscriptions," pp. 103-14.

20. See Yadin, *Masada*, pp. 108-9 and Yadin, *Ben Sira Scroll from Masada*.

21. Yigael Yadin, *Bar-Kokhba, The Rediscovery of the Legendary Hero of the Last Jewish Revolt against Imperial Rome* (London: Weldenfeld & Nicolson, 1971); Pierre Benoit, J. T. Milik, and Roland de Vaux, *Discoveries in the Judaean Desert of Jordan*, vol. 2 *Les grottes de Murabba'at* (Oxford: Clarendon Press, 1961), the second is in considerable detail.

22. Ya 'akov Meshorer, *Jewish Coins of the Second Temple Period*, trans. I. H. Levine (Tel Aviv: Am Hassefer, 1967), pp. 92-101.

23. Yadin, *Bar-Kokhba*, p. 137.

24. Herbert Danby, ed. and trans., *The Mishnah* (Oxford: Clarendon Press, 1933).

25. Frank Moore Cross, "Papyri of the Fourth Century B.C. from Daliyeh," in David Noel Freedman and Jonas C. Greenfield, eds., *New Directions in Biblical Archaeology,* 2d ed. (Garden City, N.Y.: Doubleday, 1971), pp. 45-69. In more detail see Paul W. Lapp and Nancy L. Lapp, eds., *Discoveries in the Wadi ed-Daliyeh,* vol. 41 (Cambridge: American Schools of Oriental Research, 1974).

26. Lawrence T. Geraty, "Khirbet el-Kom Bilingual Ostracon,' *BASOR,* 220 (1975), 55-62. See also "Third-Century B.C. Ostraca from Khirbet el-Kom," *HTR,* 65 (1972), 595-96 disser. abstract); and Lawrence T. Geraty, "Third-Century B.C. Ostraca from Khirbet el-Kom" (Ph.D. disser., Harvard University, 1972). Translations are the authors', not Geraty's. In this connection we must mention that Aramaic ostraca of the fourth century are known from Arad in the Negev.

27. Vasilios Tzaferis, "The Burial of Simon the Temple Builder," in *Jerusalem Revealed,* pp. 71-72. Another famous Aramaic inscription of the first century B.C.E.-C.E, but on a plaque, refers to King Uzziah: "Here were brought the bones of Uzziah, King of Judah, and do not open!" (or: ". . . and not to be opened!"). See *Inscriptions Reveal Documents from the Time of the Bible, The Mishna and the Talmud,* Exhibition Catalogue, Israe Museum Jerusalem, (winter 1973), p. 120 (English section), also illustrated in *Jerusalem Revealed,* p. 8. The reburial of Uzziah is strong indication of the growing veneration of past heroes in the Jewish tradition. See below, pp. 92ff., 155-60.

28. See note 5, above.

29. Michael Avi-Yonah, ed., *Encyclopedia of Archaeological Excavations in the Holy Land,* vol. 2 (Englewood Cliffs, N.J.: Prentice-Hall 1975), p. 634, no. 8, "Jerusalem."

30. *Ibid.,* p. 635, no. 12.

31. Joseph Naveh, "A New Tomb-Inscription from Giv'at Hamivtar," in *Jerusalem Revealed,* pp. 73-74.

32. Yadin, *Bar-Kokhba,* p. 189.

33. Yadin, *Masada.*

34. Yadin, *Bar-Kokhba,* p. 181: "It is interesting that the earlier documents are written in Aramaic while the later ones are in Hebrew. Possibly the change was made by a special decree of Bar-Kokhba who wanted to restore Hebrew as the official language of the state."

35. *Ibid.,* pp. 222-53.

36. E.g., Hengel, *Judaism and Hellenism.*

37. See note 26, above. Translations are again the authors'.

38. Fitzmyer, "Languages of Palestine in the First Century A.D." p. 508; Baruch Lifshitz, "Beiträge zur Palästinischen Epigraphik," *Zeitschrift des deutschen Palästina-Vereins,* 78 (1962), 64 ff.

39. W. H. Landau, ' A Greek Inscription Found near Hefzibah " *IEJ,* 11 (1961), 54-70.

40. W. H. Landau, "A Greek Inscription for Acre," *IEJ,* 11 (1961), 118-26; J. Schwartz, "Note complementaire a propos d'une inscription grecque de St.

Jean d'Acre," *ibid.*, 12 (1962), 135ff.; Baruch Lifshitz, "Sur la culte dynastique des Seleucides," RB, 70 (1963), pp. 75ff; A. D. Tushingham, "A Hellenistic Inscription from Samaria-Sebaste," *PEQ,* 104 (1972), 59-63.

41. *Supplementum Epigraphicum Graecum* (London, 1923–58), 19:904; 20:413.

42. *Ibid.*, 18:622.

43. *Ibid.*, 8:95.

44. *Ibid.*, 8:96.

45. *Ibid.*, 8:247-51; Eliezer Oren, "The Caves of the Palestinian Shepheleh," *Archaeology,* 18 (1965), 218-24.

46. Wilhelm Dittenberger, *Orientis Graeci inscriptiones selectae* (Leipzig: Hirzel, 1903–5), no. 415.

47. L. Y. Rahmani, "Jason's Tomb," *IEJ,* 17 (1967), 61-100; see also Avi-Yonah, *Encyclopedia of Archaeological Excavations in the Holy Land,* vol. 2, pp. 630-31.

48. J. H. Charlesworth, *The Pseudepigrapha and Modern Research,* Septuagint and Cognate Studies 7 (Missoula, Mont.: Scholars Press, 1976).

49. Josephus, *Complete Works,* trans. William Whiston (Grand Rapids: Baker Books, 1960, [1867]).

50. Josephus, *Life* 12, 17, 35, 37, 54, 65, 70, and 74. Emil Schuerer, *The History of the Jewish People in the Age of Jesus Christ (175 B.C.–A.D. 135),* rev. and ed. Geza Vermes and Fergus Millar, vol. 1 (Edinburgh: T. & T. Clark, 1973), pp. 34-37.

51. Avi-Yonah, *Encyclopedia of Archaeological Excavations in the Holy Land,* vol. 2, pp. 634-35; Nahman Avigad, "A Depository of Inscribed Ossuaries in the Kidron Valley," *IEJ,* 12 (1962), pp. 1-12, ossuaries discovered in 1941.

52. *Ibid.*, p. 631; Nahman Avigad, *EI,* 8 (1967), 119-25 (Heb.).

53. This has been published many times. Text appears in Finegan, *Archaeology of the New Testament,* pp. 119-20, with bibliography.

54. S. J. Simons, *Jerusalem in the Old Testament: Researches and Theories* (Leiden: E. J. Brill, 1952), pp. 75-76.

55. This inscription was first published by Franz Cumont, "Un rescrit imperial sur la violation de sepulture," *Revue Historique,* 163 (1930), 241-66. See also Stephan Loesch, *Diatagma Kaisaros: Die Inschrift von Nazareth und das Neue Testament* (Freiburg i. Br.: Herder, 1936). The standard edition of the text with Latin translation and bibliography appears in S. Riccobono, *Fontes iuris romani ante-justiniani,* part 1: *Leges* (Florence, 1941); and F. F. Bruce, *New Testament History* (London: Oliphants, 1971), pp. 300-303; see also Fitzmyer, "The Languages of Palestine in the First Century A.D.," p. 512, and his n. 44.

56. Benjamin Mazar, *Beth She'arim: Report on the Excavations during 1936–1940,* vol. 1: *Catacombs 1–4* (Jerusalem: Masada Press, 1973); Moshe Schwabe and Baruch Lifshitz, *Beth She'arim,* vol. 2: *The Greek Inscriptions* (Jerusalem: Masada Press, 1974); Nahman Avigad, *Beth She'arim: Report on the Excavations During 1953–1958,* vol. 3: *Catacombs 12–23* (Jerusalem: Israel Exploration Society, 1976).

57. Yadin, *Bar-Kokhba,* p. 130 for partial text, and p. 131 for illustration.

58. A. Frova, "L'iscrizione de Ponzio Pilata a Cesarea," *Rendiconti dell' istituto Lombardo, Accademia de Scienze e Lettere*, cl. di lettere, 95 (1961), pp. 419-34; Jerry Vardaman, "A New Inscription Which Mentions Pilate as 'Prefect,' " *JBL*, 81 (1962), 70-71.

59. Mazar, "The Archaeological Excavations near the Temple Mount," p. 33.

60. Finegan, *Archaeology of the New Testament*, p. 77.

61. Baruch Lifshitz, "Inscriptions latines de Cesaree (Caesarea Palestinae)," *Latomus*, 22 (1963), 783-84, reproduced in Fitzmyer, "The Languages of Palestine in the First Century A.D.," p. 505.

62. Lee I. Levine, *Caesarea Under Roman Rule*, vol. 7 (Leiden: E. J. Brill, 1975), p. 37; K. Zangemeister, "Inschrift der Vespasianischen Coloni Caesarea in Palästina," *ZDPV*, 13 (1980), 25-30.

63. Levine, *Caesarea under Roman Rule*, pp. 36-38; Joseph Ringel, "Deux nouvelles inscriptions de l'aqueduc de Cesaree maritime," *RB*, 91 (1974), 597-600. Latin epitaphs of Roman soldiers are known from many sites, e.g., old Jaffa inside Tel Aviv.

64. The known Greek materials from this region include the Qatsiyon inscription, a bilingual from Firim, two pieces of Greek from the authors' excavations at Gush Halav, and an inscribed storage jar from Meiron, also from their regional excavations. While the Jewish sites from the Golan produced no Greek inscriptional material, so much in Greek has been found in neighboring Christian and pagan sites from the same period that it would not be surprising should some Jewish Greek turn up in the future However, a similar linguistic conservatism appears to be at work here as well.

5. Jewish Burial Practices and Views of Afterlife, and Early Christian Evidences

1. E. R. Goodenough, *Jewish Symbols in the Greco-Roman Period*, vol. 1 (New York: Bollingen, 1953), pp. 61-177.

2. For the Beth She 'arim reports see above, chapter 4, n. 56.

3. The definitive essay on this subject is by Saul Lieberman, " Some Aspects of After Life in Early Rabbinic Literature," published as the Wolfson Jubilee volume (Jerusalem: American Academy for Jewish Research 1965), vol. 1, pp. 495-532.

4. M. Avi-Yonah in *Oriental Art in Roman Palestine* (Rome: Centro di Studi Semitica, Istituto di Studi del vicino oriente, Universita', 1961), pp. 65ff.

5. See. E. M. Meyers, *Jewish Ossuaries: Reburial and Rebirth* (Rome: Biblical Institute Press, 1971), esp. pp. 74-82.

6. *Ibid.*, pp. 3-12 and his article "Tomb," in *The Interpreter's Dictionary of the Bible, Supplementary Volume* (Nashville: Abingdon, 1976), pp. 905-8.

7. For the former see E. Meyers, C. Meyers, and J. F. Strange, "Excavations at Ancient Meiron, 1974–1975: Second Preliminary Report," *Annual of the American Schools of Oriental Research*, 43 (1978), 73-108, and in particular the skeletal report of Pat Smith therein; for the latter, see E. M.

Meyers, A. T. Kraabel, and J. F. Strange, *Ancient Synagogue Excavations at Khirbet Shema'* (Durham: Duke University Press, 1976), pp. 119-45.

8. Meyers, *Jewish Ossuaries,* pp. 15, 88-89, and citations there.

9. See J. F. Strange, "Crucifixion, Methods of," in *The Interpreter's Dictionary of the Bible, Supplementary Volume,* pp. 199-200.

10. Samuel Safrai and Menahem Stern, eds., *The Jewish People in the First Century,* vol. 2 (Philadelphia: Fortress Press, 1974), p. 776, n. 3.

11. This garment is called a *kliva* (*b. Moed Qat.* 27b; *t. Nid.* 9.16). Burial shrouds were usually referred to as *tachrichin.* The fact that the Gospels are not consistent in their use of Greek terms for burial shrouds may indicate confusion as to the garment actually used, the terms being *sindon* (Mark 15:46) or *othonia* (Luke 24:12).

11a. For Abraham see Gen. 25:8; Isaac, 35:9; Jacob, 49:33. The case of Joseph is especially interesting because Moses took the bones of Joseph with him to Palestine after first embalming him (Exod. 13:19). For a discussion of this point of view from a broader perspective see E. M. Meyers, *Jewish Ossuaries,* pp. 12-21.

11b. *Ibid.*

11c. J. A. T. Robinson, "Resurrection in the New Testament," in *The Interpreter's Dictionary of the Bible,* ed. by G. A. Buttrick, vol. R-Z, 1962, pp. 43-53; O. Cullmann, *Immortality of the Soul or Resurrection of the Dead,* 1958; E. W. Saunders, "Resurrection in the NT," in *The Interpreter's Dictionary of the Bible, Supplementary Volume,* ed. by K. Crim, 1976, pp. 739-41; R. H. Fuller, *The Formation of the Resurrection Narratives* (New York: Macmillan, 1971).

12. Nahman Avigad and Benjamin Mazar, "Beth She 'arim," in Michael Avi-Yonah, ed., *Encyclopedia of Archaeological Excavations in the Holy Land,* vol. 1 (Englewood Cliffs, N.J.: Prentice-Hall, 1975), p. 245.

13. See Senzo Nagakubo, "Investigations into Jewish Concepts of Afterlife in the Beth She 'arim Greek Inscriptions" (Ph.D. disser. Duke University, 1974), pp. 243-44.

14. For a critical review of the Capernaum reports see J. F. Strange's review in *BASOR,* 226 (1977), 65-73.

15. For an exhaustive review of this issue see Robert Houston Smith, "The Cross Marks on Jewish Ossuaries," *PEQ,* (1974), 53-75 and the literature cited therein.

16. *Ibid.,* n. 3-5.

17. *Ibid.,* p. 65. This is also the conclusion of L. Y. Rahmani in his recently completed Ph.D. disser. on Jewish ossuaries submitted to the Hebrew University of Jerusalem.

18. Meyers, *Jewish Ossuaries,* pp. 64-69.

19. R. H. Smith, "A Sarcophagus from Pella: New Light on Earliest Christianity," *Archaeology,* 26 (1973), 250-57.

20. See the excellent discussion of John Wilkinson in his *Jerusalem as Jesus Knew It: Archaeology as Evidence* (London: Thames and Hudson, 1978), pp. 180-94.

21. Magen Broshi, "Evidence of Earliest Christian Pilgrimage to the Holy Land Comes to Light in Holy Sepulchre Church," *BAR,* 3 (1977), 42-44. See

also the sigificant work on this subject by John Wilkinson, *Jerusalem Pilgrims Before the Crusades* (Warminster, Eng.: Aris & Phillips, 1978).

22. See Vasilios Tzaferis, "Christian Symbols of the Fourth Century and the Church Fathers" (Ph.D. disser. directed by M. Avi-Yonah, Hebrew University, 1971).

23. Ernest Saunders, "Christian Synagogues and Jewish Christianity in Galilee," *Explor.* 3 (1977), 70-78.

24. Bellarmino Bagatti, *Excavations in Nazareth*, vol. 1: *From the Beginning till the XII Century* (Jerusalem: Franciscan Press, 1969).

25. Meyers, Kraabel, and Strange, *Ancient Synagogue Excavations at Khirbet Shema'; Meyers*. Meyers, and Strange, "Excavations at Ancient Meiron, 1974–1975"; and *idem,* forthcoming Gush Halav Preliminary Report, *BASOR,* 233 (1979), 33-58.

26. Bagatti, *Excavations in Nazareth,* vol. I, p. 173.

27. The same phenomenon is to be observed at Capernaum; see Emmanuele Testa, *Cafarnao IV: I Graffiti della casa de San Pietro,* publication of the Studium Biblicum Franciscanum, no. 19 (Jerusalem: Franciscan Press, 1972).

28. Bagatti, *Excavations in Nazareth,* p. 116, fig. 70.

29. "Christian Synagogues and Jewish Christianity in Galilee," Saunders, p. 74.

6. Evidences of Early Christianity: Churches in the Holy Land

1. See chapter 5, pp. 103-8.

2. See, John G. Gager, *Kingdom and Community: The Social World of Early Christianity* (Englewood Cliffs, N.J.: Prentice-Hall, 1975); Gerd Theissen, *Sociology of Early Palestinian Christianity* (Philadelphia: Fortress Press, 1978); and especially the recent work of Wayne Meeks and Robert L. Wilken, *Jews and Christians in Antioch in the First Four Centuries of the Common Era* (Missoula: Scholars Press, 1978), which emerged out of the Working Group on the Social World of Early Christianity of the Society of Biblical Literature.

3. This is Theissen's phrase.

4. Asher Ovadiah, *Corpus of Byzantine Churches in the Holy Land* (Bonn: Peter Hanstein, 1970); and John Wilkinson, *Jerusalem Pilgrims Before the Crusades* (Warminster, Eng.: Aris & Phillips, 1978). See also Asher Ovadiah, "The Byzantine Church in Israel," *Qadmoniot,* 9 (1976), 6-16; this special issue of *Qadmoniot* is devoted entirely to the subject of churches.

5. Wilkinson, *Jerusalem Pilgrims,* pp. 173-74.

6. Ovadiah, *Corpus of Byzantine Churches,* pp. 131-33; Eusebius *Il labaro ed il sogno miracoloso nella Vita Constantini* 3.52-53.

7. Wilkinson, *Jerusalem Pilgrims,* pp. 169-70 ("Seven Springs"); Ovadiah, *Corpus of Byzantine Churches,* pp. 56-59.

8. Wilkinson, *ibid.;* Ovadiah, pp. 59-60.

9. Ovadiah, p. 56; Wilkinson, *Egeria's Travels* (London: SPCK, 1971), pp. 196-200.

10. Wilkinson, p. 173; Ovadiah, p. 71.

11. Wilkinson, p. 172; Ovadiah, pp. 140-42.

12. Wilkinson, pp. 156, 168, 172; Ovadiah, pp. 63-65, 102, 124-25.

13. Wilkinson, *Jerusalem Pilgrims*, pp. 153, 155, 165, 169, 174.

14. Wilkinson, *Egeria's Travels*, p. 202; Wilkinson, *Jerusalem Pilgrims*, p. 151.

15. Wilkinson, *Jerusalem Pilgrims*, pp. 51, 158; idem, *Egeria's Travels*, pp. 186-87. Jerome does not mention the church as such. See Joachim Jeremias, *Heiligen Gräber in Jesu Umwelt* (Göttingen: Vanderhoeck & Ruprecht, 1958), pp. 38-40, 48-49.

16. Wilkinson, *Jerusalem Pilgrims*, p. 166; Ovadiah, *Corpus of Byzantine Churches*, pp. 114-16; James L. Kelso and D. C. Baramki, *Excavations at New Testament Jericho and Khirbet en-Nitla* (New Haven: American Schools of Oriental Research, 1955), pp. 29-30.

17. Wilkinson, *Egeria's Travels*, pp. 91-98; Wilkinson, *Jerusalem Pilgrims*, p. 171.

18. See chapter 8.

19. Virgilio Corbo, *Cafarnao I: Gli edifici della citta*, publication del Studium Biblicum Franciscanum, no. 19 (Jerusalem: Franciscan Press, 1975), p. 106.

20. *Ibid.*

21. Stanislao Loffreda, *Cafarnao II: La Ceramica* (Jerusalem: Franciscan Press, 1974), p. 117.

22. See above pp. 56-58.

23. Bellarmino Bagatti, *Excavations in Nazareth*, vol. 1: *From the Beginning till the XII Century* (Jerusalem: Franciscan Press, 1969), pp. 77-218.

24. *Ibid.*, pp. 97-100.

25. *Ibid.*, pp. 100-103, 174-218.

26. *Ibid.*, p. 100, and fig. 53 on p. 98.

27. *Ibid.*, p. 16; William Smith and Henry Wace, eds., *A Dictionary of Christian Biography*, vol. 1 (London: J. Murray, 1877–87), p. 621.

28. Bagatti, *Excavations in Nazareth*, vol. 1, fig. 151, pl. IX-X, figs. 154-56, pp. 196-99. Also treated by Emmanuele Testa, *Nazaret Giudeo-Christiana, Riti, Iscrizioni, Simboli* (Jerusalem: Franciscan Press, 1969), pp. 112-23.

29. The issue of churches over caves is addressed extensively by Bellarmino Bagatti, *The Church from the Circumcision: History and Archaeology of the Judaeo-Christians*, publication of the Stadium Biblicum Franciscanum, Collectio Minor, no. 2 (Jerusalem: Franciscan Press, 1971), pp. 112-36. See also Emmanuele Testa, "Le 'Grotte dei misteri' giudeo-cristiane," *LA*, 14 (1964), 65-144; Emmanuele Testa "Le cene del Signore," *Terra Sancta* (1964), 311-16.

30. Bagatti, *Excavations in Nazareth*, vol. 1, pp. 119-23; Testa, *Nazaret Guideo-Christiana*, pp. 10-53.

31. It is noteworthy that this installation has no drain, which, in some quarters, would disqualify it from being a *mikveh*.

32. Bagatti, *Excavations in Nazareth*, vol. 1, pp. 127-29.

33. *Ibid.*, pp. 93-97, 105-8.

34. *Ibid.*, pp. 138-46 and figs. 84-97.

35. *Ibid.*, pp. 156-58 and fig. 110; Testa, *Nazaret Guidec-Cristiana*, pp. 75-76.

36. Wilkinson, *Egeria's Travels*, p. 193.

37. *Ibid.*, see note 3.

38. D. H. Kallner-Amiran, "A Revised Earthquake Catalogue of Palestine, I," *IEJ*, 1 (1950–51), 223-46. The synagogue was oriented north-south originally, if it followed the pattern of almost all other Galilean synagogues so far surveyed or exchanged.

39. Bagatti, *Excavations in Nazareth*, vol. 1, pp. 172-73.

40. *Ibid.*, pp. 219-33; Testa, *Nazaret Guideo-Cristiana*, pp. 10-22.

41. Testa, *Nazaret Guideo-Cristiana*.

42. Prosper Viaud, *Nazareth et ses deux eglises de l'Annonciction et de Saint Joseph d'apres les fouilles recents* (Paris: Picard, 1910). For a short summary see Donato Baldi and Bellarmino Bagatti, "Il Santuario della Nutrizione a Nazret," *Studi Francescani*, 9 (1937), 258-62.

43. Wilhem Schneemelcher and E. Hannecke, eds., *New Testament Apocrypha*, vol. 1: *Gospels and Related Writings*, trans. R. McL. Wilson (London: Lutterworth Press, 1963–65), pp. 370-37; the quotation is from p. 383.

44. See above, n. 29.

45. Pierre Benoit and M. E. Boismard, "Un ancien sanctuaire chretien a Bethani," *RB*, 58 (1951), 200-251; Bagatti, *The Church from the Circumcision*, pp. 134-36.

46. This would accord well with the view of Richard Krautheimer, *Early Christian and Byzantine Architecture* (Princeton University Press, 1975), p. 3, who argues that before 200 c.e. "a Christian architecture did not and could not exist. . . . Christian congregations prior to 200 were limited to the realm of domestic architecture."

7. Synagogues, Art, and the World of the Sages

1. On this subject, and for a convenient bibliographical review, see Julius Gutmann, *The Synagogue: Studies in Origins, Archaeology and Architecture* (New York: Ktav Publishing House, 1975), pp. x-xiv, 72-78. The standard older treatment on this general matter is Eliezer Lipa Sukenik, *Ancient Synagogues in Palestine and Greece* (Milford: Oxford University Press, 1934).

2. Unfortunately, these four sites are only provisionally reported; hence, no detailed study has yet emerged relating these structures to the later third- and fourth-century buildings. For a preliminary evaluation of Masada and Herodium see Gideon Foerster, "The Synagogues at Masada and Herodium," *EI*, 2 (1973), 224-28 (Heb.).

3. John Wilkinson in "Christian Pilgrims in Jerusalem During the Byzantine Period," *PEQ* (1976), 76-77 and fig. 1, prefers the number 365. In our view, however, this is highly exaggerated and avoids the question of the precise nature of the synagogue.

4. Gutmann, *The Synagogue*, pp. 74-76.

5. *Ibid.*, but see also E. Meyers, A. T. Kraabel, and J. F. Strange, *Ancient Synagogue Excavations at Khirbet Shema'* (Durham: Duke University Press, 1976), p. 87 and notes.

6. Meyers, Kraabel, and Strange, *Ancient Synagogue Excavations at Khirbet Shema'*, p. 259.

7. The two major works are Samuel Krauss, *Synagogue Altertümer* (Berlin: B. Harz, 1922), and his more general work; *Talmudische Archaeologie*, vols. 1 and 2 (Leipzig: G. Fock, 1910–11), and vol. 3 (Frankfurt: Kauffmann, 1912). But see also the recent work of F. Hüttenmeister and G. Reeg, *Die Antiken Synagogen in Israel* (Wiesbaden: L. Reichert, 1977).

8. In this regard see M. Avi-Yonah, "Editor's Note," *IEJ*, 23 (1973), 43-45, and Gideon Foerster, "Notes on Recent Excavations at Capernaum," *IEJ*, 21 (1971), 207-11.

9. Samuel Safrai, "Was There a Woman's Gallery in the Synagogue," *Tarbiz*, 32 (1969), 329-38 (Heb.).

10. See Foerster, "The Synagogues at Masada and Herodium."

11. E. Meyers, C. Meyers, J. Strange, the "Excavations at Ancient Meiron in Upper Galilee, 1974–1975: Second Preliminary Report," *AASOR*, 43 (1978), 86-87, figs. 11, 12.

12. Rachel Hachlili, "The Niche and the Ark in Ancient Synagogues," *BASOR*, 223 (1976), 43-53.

13. See J. F. Strange, "Capernaum," in *The Interpreter's Dictionary of the Bible, Supplementary Volume* (Nashville: Abingdon, 1976), pp. 140-41.

14. Nahman Avigad and Benjamin Mazar, "Beth She'arim," in M. Avi-Yonah, ed., *Encyclopedia of Archaeological Excavations in the Holy Land*, vol. 1 (Englewood Cliffs, N.J: Prentice-Hall, 1975), 233-34.

14a. John Wilkinson, *Egeria's Travels* (London: SPCK, 1971), pp. 196-200.

15. A. Thomas Kraabel, "Ancient Synagogues," in *New Catholic Encyclopedia Supplement*, vol. 16 (Washington, D.C.: Publishers Guild, 1947), p. 438.

16. As noted by M. Avi-Yonah, "Ancient Synagogues," *Ariel*, 32 (1973), 41, reprinted in Gutmann, *The Synagogue*, p. 107.

17. E. Meyers, "Synagogue Architecture," in *The Interpreter's Dictionary of the Bible, Supplementary Volume* (Nashville: Abingdon, 1976), pp. 253-54; and E. Meyers, C. Meyers, and J. F. Strange, "Preliminary Report in the 1977–1978 Excavations at Gush Halav," *BASOR*, 233 (1979), 33-58.

18. Heinrich Kohl and Carl Watzinger, *Antike Synagogen in Galilaea* (Leipzig: Hinrichs, 1916; reprinted Jerusalem: Kedem, 1973), plate xv.

19. Avi-Yonah, "Ancient Synagogues," p. 32; Meyers, "Synagogue Architecture," pp. 842-45.

20. Meyers, Kraabel and Strange, *Ancient Synagogue Excavations at Khirbet Shema'*, pp. 37-39.

21. As quoted by J. Baumgarten, "Art in the Synagogue: Some Talmudic Views," *Judaism*, 19 (1970), 197.

22. An excellent discussion of this attitude can be found in Carmel Konikoff, *The Second Commandment and Its Interpretation in the Art of Ancient Israel* (Geneva: Imprimerie du Journal de Geneve, 1973), pp. 89ff.; this work also includes a compendious bibliography on the subject, pp. 101-13.

23. Rachel Hachlili, "The Zodiac in Ancient Jewish Art," *BASOR*, 228 (1977), 61-77.

23a. R. Bultmann, *History of the Synoptic Tradition* (New York: Harper, 1963), p. 282, calls this an example of *"purely novelistic motifs"* (his emphasis). Cf. also W. F. Albright and C. S. Mann, *Matthew: A New Translation with Introduction and Commentary*, The Anchor Bible, vol. 26 (Garden City, N.Y.: Doubleday, 1971), p. 351, who call it "a dramatization of a saying preserved in the Johannine tradition."

8. Jewish and Christian Attachment to Palestine

1. William D. Davies, *The Gospel and the Land: Early Christianity and Jewish Territorial Doctrine* (Berkeley: University of California Press, 1974).

2. See Dennis E. Groh, "Galilee and the Eastern Roman Empire in Late Antiquity," *Explor*, 3 (1977), 78-93 and E. M. Meyers, J. F. Strange, and D. E. Groh, "The Meiron Excavation Project: Archaeological Survey in Galilee and Golan, 1976," *BASOR*, 230 (1978), 18-22.

3. One reason for this situation may be the paucity of scholarship on the Palestinian Talmud in English and the preeminent position that the Babylonian Talmud enjoys in rabbinic scholarship. With the focus of talmudic scholarship to this day upon the Babylonian Talmud, it is understandable that most students of the period would tend to focus on the creative genius of the Babylonian sages. M. Avi-Yonah's *The Jews of Palestine* (New York: Schocken, 1976), an English revision of the German and Hebrew editions, goes a long way in countering this impression.

4. Frank Moore Cross's programmatic essay "Aspects of Samaritan and Jewish History in Late Persian and Hellenistic Times," *HTR*, 59 (1966), 201-11, places the discussion of the Second Temple Diaspora in the appropriate context of dialogue and strife with Jerusalem.

5. Gerson Cohen, "Zion in Rabbinic Literature," in *Zion in Jewish Literature*, ed. A. S. Halkin (New York: Herzel Press, 1961). p. 39.

6. As quoted by Cohen, *ibid.*, p. 40, from *Wayyikra Rabbc* 13.2.

7. See above, n. 3. The enormous work of Jacob Neusner on the Babylonian community, *A History of the Jews of Babylonia*, 5 vols. (Leiden: E. J. Brill, 1965–70), has rightly brought attention to the eastern Semitic world of the sages. For a review of the evidence for synagogues in the Diaspora, see the forthcoming work of A. T. Kraabel, "The Diaspora Synagogue: Archaeological and Epigraphic Evidence since Sukenik," in *Aufstieg und Niedergang der Römischen Welt*, ed. H. Temporini and W. Haase (forthcoming).

8. On pilgrimage in Judaism see the several works of Samuel Safrai, "Relations between the Diaspora and the Land of Israel," in *Compendia*, vol. I, pp. 184-215; and his *Pilgrimage at the Time of the Second Temple* (Tel Aviv: Am Hassefer, 1965) (Heb.).

9. As quoted by Cohen, "Zion in Rabbinic Literature," p. 43, from *b. Sota* 14a.

10. See Benjamin Mazar, *Beth She'arim: Report on the Excavations During 1936–1940*, vol. 1: *Catacombs 1–4* (Jerusalem: Masada Press, 1973), pp. 6-7, where the date of 352 c.e. is given for the destruction of Beth She'arim.

11. For a discussion of the date and context of this prayer see the authoritative work of Joseph Heinemann, *Prayer in the Talmud: Forms and Patterns* (Berlin: de Gruyter, 1977); and Cohen, "Zion in Rabbinic Literature," pp. 54-58.

12. See Y. Gafni's discussion of this issue (which includes some comment on E. Meyers, *Jewish Ossuaries: Reburial and Rebirth* [Rome: Biblical Institute Press, 1971]), in "On the Origin of Bringing the Deceased from Abroad for Burial in Eretz Israel," *Cathedra,* 4 (1977), 113-20 (Heb.). The views of Meyers are conveniently summarized in "The Theological Implications of an Ancient Jewish Burial Custom," *JQR,* 62 (1971), 95-119.

13. *T. Abod. Zar.* 4.3; *b.Ketub.* 111a; and *Abot R. Nat.,* ed. Schechter, Text A, p. 82.

14. *Gen. Rab.* 96.5 and *y. Kil.* 9.3.

15. See, e.g., the works of Gerd Theissen and John G. Gager cited in chapter 6, n. 2.

16. For a classic statement of symbolism in the Gospel of John see Charles H. Dodd, *The Interpretation of the Fourth Gospel* (Cambridge University Press, 1953), pp. 133-43.

17. Charles K. Barrett, *The Gospel According to St. John: An Introduction with Commentary and Notes on the Greek Text* (London: SPCK, 1955), p. 211.

18. William H. Brownlee, "Whence the Gospel According to John?" in *John and Qumran,* ed. James H. Charlesworth (London: Geoffrey Chapman, 1972), pp. 166-94, esp. p. 169.

19. Egeria wished to visit Aenon and was directed to a garden two hundred yards from Sedima (Salim) by her guide, a monk. She was interested in the "Salem" of Melchisedek but remembered the Aenon near Salim where John was baptizing. See John Wilkinson, *Egeria's Travels,* Newly Translated with Supporting Documents and Notes (London: SPCK, 1971), pp. 110-11.

20. Erich Klostermann, ed., *Das Onomstikon der biblischen Ortsnamen,* Eusebius: *Werke* 3/i, vol. 11, part 1 of *Die griechischen Christlichen Schriftsteller der ersten drei Jahrhunderte* (Hildesheim: Georg Olms, 1966, a reprint of the Leipzig: Hinrichs, 1904 ed.), p. 116.

21. Charles H. Dodd, *Historical Tradition in the Fourth Gospel* (Cambridge University Press, 1963).

22. Joachim Jeremias, *Heiligen Graeber in Jesu Umwelt: Eine Untersuchung zur Volksreligion der Zeit Jesu* (Göttingen: Vanderhoeck & Ruprecht, 1958).

23. *Ibid.,* pp. 11-13.

24. Charles Cutler Torrey, *The Lives of the Prophets: Greek Text and Translation* (Philadelphia: Society of Biblical Literature and Exegesis, 1946); Jeremias, *Heiligen Graeber in Jesu Umwelt,* pp. 11-12.

25. Wilkinson, *Egeria's Travels,* pp. 153-63.

26. *Ibid.,* p. 89-150.

27. *Ibid.,* pp. 179-210.

28. *Ibid.*

29. John Wilkinson, *Jerusalem Pilgrims Before the Crusades* (Warminster, Eng.: Aris & Phillips, 1977), p. 35.

Glossary

APSE: The rounded end of a church or synagogue in which area the focus of worship was directed.

ARCOSOLIUM: An elaboration of a *loculus* whereby its roof is carved into an arch. The burial niches or *loculi* are set into the recessed arch either perpendicularly or horizontally and are usually intended for primary interments.

BEMA: A raised platform in the Jewish synagogue from which Scripture was read and interpreted and over which a receptacle for the scrolls was located.

DUNAM: A plot of land of 1,000 square meters, approximately one quarter of an acre. The term was introduced into the Middle East in colonial times.

EARLY CHRISTIANITY: A blanket term for the early Christian movement in all its variety in the many localities where it took root in the Roman Empire and beyond. In this text we use it to designate pre-Constantinian Christianity. The term makes no judgment as to the ethnic identity of the people involved.

EARLY PALESTINIAN JUDAISM: Refers to the formative period in Jewish history from the latter Hasmonaeans until Rabbi Judah the Patriarch, c. 200 C.E.

ERETZ ISRAEL: Literally "the Land of Israel" in Hebrew. A term from the Bible (I Sam. 13:19; II Kings 5:2) with variable meaning, but used from the first century B.C.E. onward to designate the total territory once inhabited by Israelites. See *Holy Land, Palestine.*

GENTILE CHRISTIANITY: Refers to those of Gentile birth who came to believe in the Messiahship of Jesus. Carries the connotation of "Hellenized" among scholars.

HELLENIZATION: The process whereby Greek language and ideas are appropriated into a non-Greek society. In ancient *Palestine* this process was accelerated by the conquest of Alexander the Great (c. 330 B.C.E.), the translation of Hebrew Scripture into Greek (the Septuagint, early third century B.C.E.), and the incorporation of *Palestine* into the Roman Empire (after 63 B.C.E.).

HOLY LAND: A pilgrim term reflecting the exalted status of the area of *Palestine,* or *Eretz Israel,* in Judaism and Christianity. It usually denotes the same territory as "Palestine" or "Eretz Israel."

JEWISH CHRISTIANITY: Refers to early believers in the Messiahship of Jesus from among the native Palestinian Jewish population. The term came to apply to all those of Jewish birth who adopted this new faith.

LOCULUS: Also known in Aramaic as *kokh,* this is the burial niche cut into the walls of underground tomb chambers for the reception of either a primary or secondary burial. Such niches, or *loculi,* are common in catacombs. Burial in such a niche precluded using a coffin. This Semitic custom has been adopted in the West.

ORIENTAL: A term which describes certain characteristics of Near Eastern art, such as frontality, which accompanied the resurgence of local art in the classical world.

OSSUARY: Literally "bone box." A short coffin, about 80 cm. long, used in the Jewish custom of reburial of the desiccated remains of the dead known as secondary burial. These small chests are found especially in and around Jerusalem in the late Second Temple period, but have also been found in many other areas of the country and in later periods. The custom of secondary burial in Judaism persists throughout the talmudic era.

PALESTINE: A term derived from the biblical *peleshet,* meaning "Philistine." As a geographical term, it first appears in Herodotus as "the Palestine Syria." Philo in the first century C.E. equated Palestine and Canaan. It was not the official name of the area until 135 C.E., when the Romans discarded the name "Provincia Judaea"

198

in favor of "Syria Palestina." Between 358 and 400 C.E. the country was split into Palestina Prima (Judaea, Idumaea, Samaria, and Peraea) and Palestina Secunda (Galilee, Gaulanitis, and certain cities of the Decapolis). Used here synonymously with *Eretz Israel.*

PALESTINIAN CHRISTIANITY: The emerging Christian movement within the traditional borders of Palestine. Used in distinction to the more Hellenized, less traditionally Jewish congregations that grew up in the cities of the Roman Empire.

POST-BIBLICAL JUDAISM: This term is usually applied to the development of the earliest forms of Jewish expression, dating from the Babylonian Exile and Restoration in the sixth century B.C.E. and including the entire Second Temple Period (515 B.C.E.–C.E. 70) as well as the period of the rabbis (the first four or five centuries of the common era). Since the dating of the Old Testament canon is usually assigned to the Council of Jamnia (C.E. 90), and because this term includes other forms of Jewish literary expression besides Scripture, namely the rabbinic writings, it is a rather all-embracing term which has led to a good deal of confusion. Still, many scholars persist in using this term because of its joining of the later biblical era with the rabbis.

RABBINIC JUDAISM: (See also *Talmud.*) The movement within Judaism which centered about religion as interpreted and understood by the sages and rabbis, from about the late first century B.C.E. until the compilation of the two Talmuds c. 400 and 500 C.E. The rabbinic world focused upon the academy rather than the Temple, destroyed in C.E. 70, and in *Palestine* was headed by the Patriarch. The term *classical Judaism* goes beyond chronological delimitation to point to the core of the so-called normative community after the Council of Jamnia, i.e., early rabbinic Judaism as articulated by the schools which came to predominate under Yochanan ben Zakkai, Gamaliel, etc.

RESURRECTION: A Jewish belief, possibly taken over during the Persian period, in renewed life after death. While traces of such a belief are quite scant in the Hebrew Bible, it becomes the dominant view of afterlife in early Palestinian Judaism and constitutes a central theme of Jewish liturgy and philosophy. It is also the dominant belief in the early Palestinian church.

SARCOPHAGUS: A full-length, human-sized coffin utilized mainly for primary, or onetime, burial of corpses. Many of these coffins are handsomely decorated and some have been utilized as *ossuaries* for multiple secondary burials also.

SHEOL: The term in Hebrew Scripture utilized to describe the underworld, usually equated with Hades. It is pictured as dark and dingy, the place to which enervated individuals, or "souls," retire after life.

TALMUD: The major literary repository of Jewish law and lore existing in two versions, the Palestinian Talmud 400 c.e. and the Babylonian Talmud 500 c.e. The Talmud consists of two parts, *mishnah* and *gemara*. The *Mishnah* of Rabbi Judah the Patriarch, c. 200 c.e., is the oldest portion and is a Hebrew-language commentary on biblical law including much nonlegal material. Its formulators are known as *tannaim* ("repeaters"), hence the term *tannaitic Judaism*, i.e., Judaism of the first two centuries. *Gemara,* an Aramaic-language commentary on *mishnah,* is the creation of the sages, known as *amoraim* ("speakers"), hence the term *amoraic Judaism,* i.e., Judaism after 200 c.e. until the compilation of the two Talmuds.

Index

201